ADVENTURES WITH DAD

A Father and Daughter's Journey
Through A Senior Acting Class

By

Lee Gale Gruen

ISBN: 978-0-9884468-3-0
Library of Congress Control Number: 2013931763

First Published by *AuthorMike Ink*, 5/15/2013

www.AuthorMikeInk.com

AuthorMike Ink and its logo are trademarked by *AuthorMike Ink Publishing*.

Printed in the United States of America

For My Children

TABLE OF CONTENTS

Foreword   i

Preface and Acknowledgements   v

Chapter 1: The First Father/Daughter Team   1
            in Our Senior Acting Class

Chapter 2: Goodbye Mom   17

Chapter 3: The Invitation that Changed Our   37
            Lives

Chapter 4: Our First Scene: 59
            "Going to the Movies with Dad"

Chapter 5: Performing Onstage in the Class   73
            Showcase...What a High!

Chapter 6: Our Second Scene: 94
            "Going Camping with Dad"

Chapter 7: Our Third Scene: 115
            "Going to the Airport with Dad"

Chapter 8: Our Fourth Scene: 144
            "Dad Goes Mod"

Chapter 9: Our Fifth Scene: 169
            "Dad Goes Digital"

Chapter 10: Our Sixth Scene: 189
             "Going to the Market with Dad"

Chapter 11: Dad in the Nursing Home   216

Chapter 12: Goodbye Dad   231

Chapter 13: I'll Tell Ya, I Could Write a Book   250

FOREWORD

Dim the lights. Before our actors come out to perform, I hope you will find some context about them in my opening monologue. You see, Lee Gale's dad, my grandfather, needed to entertain…regularly. In my mother's own words, he often needed to be the center of attention. It seems to me that many families have a member who is like my grandfather. We had one. We loved him dearly, but one was all our family had room for. While my grandfather was "on," he really was entertaining, whether our family wanted to be entertained or not. I think his heart and mind were in the right place. As best I could tell, he thought that people constantly wanted to be entertained. If he got the sense that someone was bothered by his efforts, he would wonder what their problem was.

As my grandfather grew increasingly frail and his endurance waned, it became more difficult for him to keep it up. He would compensate by using different tricks. I remember on more than one occasion, he would tell me, his thirty-something year old grandson, in the middle of the day that I looked tired and needed to rest, so he had better let me go. Of course, I saw this for what it was and played along. I was grateful for his attention, even when limited.

As my grandfather grew older, my mother looked for ways to reach out and connect with him. She found acting for herself. Then, she took a brilliant leap to introduce him to it. Looking at it in hindsight, I think he was in his element, having acted offstage most of his life. How special it was for my mother and grandfather to engage each other onstage for real, live and eager audiences to see.

Part of what worked so well for my grandfather was that he could count on scheduled rehearsals and plan in advance for the dress rehearsals and performances. He could save his strength for when it counted. In fact, onstage acting became a source of excitement, interest and purpose for him. He was often more relaxed around our family during his acting days. Perhaps his need to entertain was finally being reliably fulfilled.

I remember my mother fretting about what turned out to be my grandfather's last performance. By that time, he was in a wheelchair. Despite multiple rehearsals, he struggled to remember all of his lines throughout the scene. I have heard it said that the fear of speaking in front of audiences is one of the most common. Perhaps that fear stems from the concern of saying or doing the wrong thing publicly, and from the embarrassment that would follow.

Nonetheless, they both braved their fears. After all, the show must go on.

I remember watching with my mother a video of the last "Adventures with Dad" performance. She grinned proudly as we sat together.

"He nailed it," she said. I was excited for them, but not surprised. Even in his later days, I think he understood the moment, the need to deliver. Lots of adrenaline didn't hurt either.

While my mother raised me, she had a career as a probation officer. She took up acting soon after she retired. At that time, neither one of us saw what it would do for her personally. This book shows how she also used acting to reach out to and connect with my grandfather in a new way, and share that newly found, father-daughter connection with audiences. I think that connection inspired her to work very hard on acting, performing, and ultimately writing this book. If you are entertained by it, my grandfather would have been happy knowing that. It would also give purpose to my mother's quest as a spry and burgeoning actor and author. I hope you enjoy it.

-The Author's Son

PREFACE AND ACKNOWLEDGMENTS

I first thought of writing this memoir as a gift to my children. As it began to develop in my mind, it seemed like such a touching and unique story that I thought the public might be interested. As it slowly and painfully took form, it became an homage to my father, sealing our special bond which blossomed when we began attending a community acting class for seniors together. That experience changed our lives so much that I now advocate for senior community programs whenever possible. I have reinvented myself in my senior years and hope to show others that they can do the same. Find your passion so you have a reason to get up in the morning, get out of bed and embrace life. I view this book as a giving-back to the community. If it can be a source of pleasure or inspiration for someone else, I will be satisfied.

Forced to write scenes to perform with my father in the class showcases, I discovered my talent for writing. Thoughts began to spill out of nowhere and culminated in my composing this account of that magical time we shared. The process has been grueling, consuming, fun, demanding, frustrating, exhilarating and an incredible growth experience. The very process of writing the book became a catharsis, allowing me to deal with the death first of my mother and, several years later, my father. It has enabled me to look at my own fears, inadequacies, and the forces that have controlled me all my life. I can now understand why therapists encourage their patients to journal. Things are so much clearer when you write them down. Feelings and memories flowed from my brain to my fingers that I never even realized I had. I have often been stunned by what I've just written. It's almost as though it has a life of its own with me trailing helplessly behind.

This is a true story which I have presented to the best of my recollection. The names of some of the people, places and other things have been changed to protect the privacy of the individuals involved.

A new door has opened for me. Never previously having written for pleasure in my life, I am now writing regularly. I attend writer's workshops, networking groups, writing critique groups, and this book is being published. Currently, I am working on my next book of memoir short stories.

I conceived the idea for this book cover a few years ago. I made a simple, pencil sketch of it which I subsequently sent to my publisher. He liked the concept and forwarded it to his book cover designer.

I want to thank Sara Espano at Enve Creative (website: envecreative.com) who transformed my idea into the beautiful book cover you see, using me as the model for the female figure on the cover.

I want to be sure to thank the special people who were instrumental along the way in making this book a reality: Barbara Gannen for being the great acting teacher she is; Buddy Powell, another wonderful acting teacher; Caroline and Jim Gerstley, my friends and prop carriers, for their help, encouragement and continual support; Maya Lopez for her friendship and her brutal honesty about my first draft; Jesse Lopez for his technical support and the hours he spent sitting with me at the computer fitting old technology photos into new technology media; author Wallace King for reading and critiquing the nascent efforts of a total stranger; photographer Audrey Stein who took the photographs which appear on the title facing page and on page 142; photographer Douglas M. Nelson who took the character headshot photographs which appear on pages 246 and 247; photographer Shandon Youngclaus who took the main headshot photograph which appears on page 245 and the author photograph which appears at the end of the book and on the back of the book cover; photographer Koi Sojer who took the photograph on page 243; my publisher Mike Aloisi for his patience, encouragement and belief in me; my daughter for helping me to become the person I am today; and my son for sharing the ups and downs with me during the writing of this book and life in general.

CHAPTER 1
The First Father/Daughter Team
in Our Senior Acting Class

It started nonchalantly with a thought I blurted out without even realizing I was saying it. It's funny how something as simple as that can change your whole life.

My father, Marvin Schelf, was probably a pretty typical father of the time. During my growing years, he was at work during the day and got home at night in time for dinner. That was followed by opening the mail and some brief talk before going to bed and starting it all over again the next day.

I never got to spend much time with Dad alone. On weekends and vacations I always had to share him with my mother, Rose, and my sister, Julie. After he retired, I was busy raising my own children and working, so there was very limited quality time with him then, either.

Dad had always seemed so powerful when I was a child. I remember how insensitive and even mean he could be if he thought he was being portrayed in a bad light.

With My Parents at Age 10

There was that time when I was about ten years old and Dad's family had been invited over for dinner. With the typical tension and anxiety at my house proceeding such an event, Mother was cooking while the rest of us were cleaning the house and setting up the folding table in the living room for the meal. Dad was a nervous, high-strung person at the best of times. He was especially so with the dinner looming, because it was always so important to him to make a good impression in front of his family, or anyone else for that matter.

While everyone was eating, Mother plunked a ladleful of oh-so-nutritious, canned peas on my plate, knowing that I hated them. As I pushed the peas around with my fork, making some semblance of eating them, Mother kept interrupting the banter around the table by imploring me to take just a few more bites. Irritated by our little drama, Dad bellowed at me in front of the entire assembly.

"Lee Gale, eat those peas."

All conversation stopped as everyone stared at me: aunts, uncles, cousins and my mother and sister. I was mortified. I lowered my head and just sat there, trying to hold back the tears.

"I said, eat those peas!" Fist banging on the table.

While they all watched, I ate the peas, one at a time, along with the tears and mucus dripping onto them from my eyes and nose. That incident stays in my mind as though it happened yesterday. It seems like such a small thing now that I look back, but to a young sensitive child, it was huge.

There was certainly the flip side of those dark memories of dinners with the extended family.

"Please can we play Pokeno (a Bingo-type of game with playing cards substituting for the traditional numbers)," begged all of us cousins in unison when we finished eating.

We'd each fight for our favorite card. Mine was the one with the Ace, King, Queen, Jack and Ten of diamonds heading the five rows. The competition was fierce–jail house and cut-throat. We protested loudly when my father announced it was going to be the last round; we could have played all night. We concentrated carefully to be the first to fill the entire card–full bragging rights to the winner.

With My Favorite Doll at Age 2

I always knew Dad loved me; there were those tender and caring moments. I have a vague memory of him laughing, hugging me and rubbing my back for a moment once when I was little and almost asleep. I felt so protected in his big arms.

So many other times Dad frightened me with his loud voice and threatening presence. I was afraid of what he might do if pushed too far. As I got older and stood up to him more and more, I was always careful never to test that limit, just like my mother and sister. We were all too scared to find out what might be on the other side. I learned that lesson well and carried it into my adulthood in all my relationships with men, be they husbands, boyfriends, bosses, teachers, whomever.

Dad had worked most of his life for a large corporation: North American Aviation when he started, it became North American Rockwell by the time he retired thirty years later. As a new employee, he began as a security guard and eventually worked himself up to a mid-level management position—not a bad trajectory for a bright man with limited qualifications.

His final job was evaluating employee suggestions for monetary awards if they might save the company money. For some reason, the title of that position had the term "engineer" attached to it. That was all Dad needed to hear. From then on, he told everyone he was an engineer. If others got the idea that he'd had a lot more education than he actually did, and maybe a college degree or two, so much the better.

Dad had never graduated from college, although he did take a few courses. Nevertheless, he was smart and self-taught in many areas. He loved to read and was always devouring a tome of some sort. I can still picture him curled up on the sofa, distance glasses on his forehead, wrapped in his worn, old robe that still had "plenty of use left in it," cupping his latest book. As a consequence, he was very well-informed about the world. He seemed to know something about almost everything. Maybe it was his self-assurance that was so persuasive. Anyhow, he was the kind of man whom you trusted when he talked because he spoke with such authority.

Dad had been an avid card player all his life. In his later years, he played Bridge regularly at the local senior citizens center where he was among the best. Bridge is a game for the cunning, calculating mind, and that described him perfectly.

I emulated Dad and learned how to play Bridge, too. It happened my last semester of college. I was so hooked that I cut classes just to sit in the Student Union at UCLA and play Bridge all day. It's a wonder I even graduated.

Once, Dad and I were summoned to jury duty at the same courthouse. We were able to request date changes so we could be there together. We spent most of our down time playing Bridge in the jury waiting room with the other devotees we met. That was a rare and special time.

Dad As a Young Man

Dad was a young man during the Great Depression, which began in the 1930's. As a consequence, he had a frugal philosophy which he delighted in passing along to his children. We always lived conservatively because, of course, he was saving

7

and investing everything he could. Where money was concerned, Dad was a cheapskate and a shrewd investor all rolled up together.

One of the main things I remember hearing from my father were his frequent monologues about money. He became interested in the stock market and bought mutual funds back when his friends and family members had never even heard of them, constantly planning for his retirement. For a man of modest financial means, he invested wisely over the years and managed to amass a rather impressive portfolio.

When I was a teenager, Dad finally gave me a paltry allowance only because Mother shamed him into doing so. However, he made certain he'd have the final word. After taking me to the bank and helping me open my first bank account, he lectured me on the importance of saving a portion of my new wealth. It was the spending-a-portion-of-it part that he couldn't quite master.

Dad even used to give Mother an allowance for her personal needs. After Julie and I were grown and Mother got her first job since before we were born, she'd give her paycheck to Dad who would deposit it in the bank and dole it out to her as he saw fit. That infuriated me when I became an adult and realized that women could control their own money. I used to argue with her about it.

"Mother, California is a community property state. You own half of everything in the family. You don't have to just sit back and accept whatever allowance he decides to give you."

"That's all right, honey. I don't need much," she'd answer wearily. "It's just easier than arguing with him."

Mother never needed much. She wore little makeup, just a touch of lipstick and eyebrow pencil. A bit on the plump side, she dressed as plainly and cheaply as she could. She never went to the beauty parlor, just clipping her dark hair into a short, sensible bob. It was probably the result of her poor upbringing. I remember her telling me that as a teenager she only had two dresses, both exactly alike. Her father was a tailor, and one day he brought home a big bolt of checked cloth and made dresses for all his daughters. I would listen to those stories, then just shrug and go about my important teenage business.

I was embarrassed by Mother's dowdy ways and used to wish she'd be more like my friends' mothers, more attractive and stylish. I still feel guilty when I remember that time in high school when there was a mother-daughter tea. When I saw my mother enter the room, I felt like cringing because she looked so frumpy. I ignored her as much as I could and just stayed close to my best friend and her mother who was so stylish with her hair done up in the latest fashion, carefully arranged by the beautician she frequented weekly.

I know Mother was very hurt. When I think of that incident, I wish so deeply that I could go back and do it differently.

Mother was also fixated on cleanliness, which was probably lacking in her childhood in a household of so many bodies and so little money. She was always cleaning. She would chastise Dad for licking his fingers while carving the dinner roast, or if he had his feet on the couch or coffee table. He would explode, mocking her with, "Always cleaning...always cleanliness."

As an elderly woman, Mother spread newspapers over the floor and flanking the stove burners in their tiny apartment kitchen to catch any possible spattering of grease. It was an obstacle course to walk into that room, slipping and sliding on the day's news. It's amazing that the burner-hugging papers didn't catch fire. Of course, there was no reasoning with Mother.

Mother and Dad used to have constant disputes about the grocery shopping. If she bought a pound of apples which he could have gotten for ten cents a pound cheaper somewhere else, the bickering would start. Mother finally just stopped doing the household shopping and Dad took it over.

Armed with the newspaper coupons he'd clip religiously, he hit every market between his job and home, buying only things on sale. Sometimes I went with him to help carry out the items he chose so carefully.

"What do you mean it's twenty-nine cents a pound," he'd typically yell at the cashier. "Don't give me that crap. The sign said twenty-five cents a pound."

That was so characteristic of our marketing trips. His raging arguments over being charged even a few pennies too much would always embarrass me. I'd shrink into myself as much as possible. Maybe no one would notice I was with him.

Why couldn't I have a father like other kids' fathers? I'd wonder.

Dad was always bragging about his job, investments and anything else that would lend itself to boasting—always inflating his own importance. His frequent hyperbole used to make me so uncomfortable as I watched it over the years. Why did he have to behave like that? I was well into my adulthood before I understood.

Dad had so many different facets to him. Way up there toward the top of the list was his value of travel, and he encouraged that passion in his children. The only things he used to splurge on were fascinating vacations.

"Mother and I are going to Europe," he announced one day.

I never knew anyone who went to Europe. That was just for the famous people in magazines and newspapers. I was always impressed with Dad for that. My father could also be a trend-setter.

When I was a child, Dad, Mother, Julie and I used to go on vacations to Yosemite National Park. We'd stay in a canvas-roofed cabin and take daily hikes.

"Tomorrow morning we'll all get up early and hike to the base of Bridal Veil Falls," Dad informed us one night as we were all bunking down.

We did, and it was beautiful. The Falls really did look like a bride's veil. We cupped our hands and drank from the pool of water at the base. On our way back, we came upon an overgrown orchard.

"Let's boil the fruit and make compote," Dad suggested after we had all filled some bags with the pears we picked.

I loved those trips. We were all so relaxed, and the constant tension at home just melted away. I hated it when we had to leave and return to the harness of our real life.

Our family trips and my parents' vacations planted the seeds for my own love of travel and nature. Throughout my life, I have explored the world and what it has to offer, just like they did.

When my parents celebrated their twentieth wedding anniversary, Dad secretly bought Mother an expensive, diamond ring. He took us all out to a restaurant for the Early Bird Special, naturally, and presented it to her. We were blown away, to say the least. Of course, he reminded us that it was also a good investment, lest we forget the value of a buck. On the way home, we stopped at a market—Dad wanted to buy some bananas that were on sale.

"How do you think I got the money for the diamond ring?" he joked when we teased him about it.

Everyone in the extended family chided Dad about being so cheap. But, he was the one who had money to support himself in his final years, never having to rely on anyone else.

He would often say, "I don't want to be beholden to my children," and he never was.

* * *

So, what was that life-changing thought I spontaneously blurted out so long ago? It was very simple, really. Shortly after my mother died, I invited my father to come with me to a senior acting class I had recently started attending, just to cheer him up.

At the beginning of our remarkable journey, I was sixty and Dad was eighty-five. Both of us were retired and alone now—Dad newly widowed and me newly divorced after a second try at marriage. Dad, portly, pale and average looking as a younger man, was thin and slightly stooped with a head full of pure white, wavy hair. I was slender with dyed-blonde, curly hair and resembled him.

Neither of us had ever acted in our lives. I had never done anything remotely similar, and the closest Dad had ever gotten was doing a few "extra" jobs a couple of years earlier.

I'd seen a notice stapled to a telephone pole about working as a movie extra. I tore off one of the paper tabs cut into a fringe on the bottom. It had the contact information, and I gave it to Dad thinking it might be fun for him in his retirement. He called to inquire and eventually signed up with the agency.

Soon, he was sent out on his first job to a very upscale home in Beverly Hills. He was supposed to be part of a party scene in the backyard around the swimming pool.

There was a large buffet table filled with scrumptious food, but it was a prop and nobody was allowed to touch any of it. Instead, they were fed some much less appetizing grub. The hours were long, the pay was poor and Dad didn't really like the experience.

Another time, he was called for an audition where he was told to dress in jeans and a tee shirt. As preparation, he'd had a haircut the day before. The morning of the audition he got up, showered and shaved, and put on a clean pair of jeans and a new white tee shirt he'd bought just for the occasion.

When he arrived at the appointed location after a long drive, all the other men there to audition were unshaven, unkempt and dressed in dirty old clothes. It seems they were casting for homeless men.

The agent called Dad for another job, but he declined. He had committed to playing Bridge that day. She was flabbergasted.

"You'd give up a day's work to play cards?"

She never called him again and that was just fine with Dad. He was sick of the whole thing.

* * *

It was just supposed to be a lark–just something to do. Soon, the two of us were driving every week to our acting class. We became the first father/daughter team in that class or, I suspect, in any other of its kind.

Slowly, without even being aware of it, acting began to dominate our every conversation and take on a life of its own. It was like a forbidden drug. We didn't fight it, didn't even want to kick the habit. We simply went wherever it took us, constantly craving more.

Dad and I started rehearsing in person or on the phone several times a day, communicating more than ever in our lives. During those three magical years, I bonded more with my father than I had in the previous sixty.

Now, here I am, in a place I had never thought about, never lusted after, never even considered appealing. How did it all come about?

CHAPTER 2
Goodbye Mother

"Well, she's gone," whispered Dad's voice over the telephone, saying the unimaginable.

Dad had become Mother's main caretaker over the past many months, and now he was alone. I knew he was devastated, even though his voice sounded in control–never show your feelings, and all that.

Mother had been going steadily downhill the past few weeks since her last fall. She had gone to the bathroom in the middle of the night, stumbled and hit her forehead on the edge of the sink.

They had only been in the new apartment building for a short time, one with an elevator. Julie and I were so happy when they'd finally agreed to move two doors down the street.

We'd had such plans. We would be able to take Mother outside in a wheelchair. She'd see the trees and kids playing. She'd talk to passersby. She loved to talk to people and watch the children. She always blossomed on those rare occasions when she got out of that prison of an apartment and reconnected with humanity.

Julie and I had been arguing with them for ages to move from the second-floor, walk-up apartment they'd lived in for twenty years. They refused, stubbornly holding onto their independence.

"Don't try to run my life," my mother would scold us, trying to preserve some control over her now feeble existence. "I'll do what I want."

Mother was a rigid, somewhat depressed woman. We always called her "Mother," never Mommy or Mom. I don't know why. That's how she must have taught us, maybe because she was denied the use of those endearing terms in her own childhood.

There was not much flexibility in my home when I was growing up. I remember when I was in grammar school how much I loved going over to my best friend's house to play after school. As it got toward dinner time she'd often ask her mother if I could stay and eat with them; the answer was always "yes." Sometimes, when my girlfriend was playing at my house, I'd ask Mother if she could stay for dinner.

"No, I only made enough for our family tonight. If you want to invite a friend for dinner, you have to ask me in advance so I can plan it."

That was my first lesson in stifling spontaneity. Being young, impulsive and never seeming to ask far enough in advance to suit my mother, I just stopped inviting friends for dinner.

That was typical in my house. There was a general uptightness in the air, a lack of ease, a choking. When I had my own children, I insisted on the put-another-cup-of-water-in-the-soup rule and just broke out cheese and crackers or anything else on hand to supplement the meal so friends could stay for dinner at the last minute. Why didn't my mother know that people and friendships are more important than food?

Mother had always been a bitter person, a result of a deprived childhood lived during World War I and its aftermath. She became more embittered as she aged. In her final years, I dreaded visiting her; it was too stressful. Most of our time together just ended with her ranting and my stomach in knots.

Mother was tiny and frail by then. She wore a wig as her own hair had thinned so much. Her usual dress was a housecoat and slippers.

She became a recluse in their old apartment, hardly able to walk up and down the stairs anymore by herself. On the rare occasions she would attempt it, usually to go to the doctor, she managed the feat by holding onto the handrail on one side and one of us on the other. She had sunk into an existence of her ailments, medicines and doctor's appointments.

After Mother's last fall, Julie called me from the hospital and told me to sit down.

"She's dying, isn't she?" I said, still standing.

"Yes," she answered in a low voice. "The doctor said there's no need to keep rushing her to the hospital every time she falls. There's nothing more they can do for her. It's nature's way."

The falls and drives to the hospital had settled into a way of life. Now, everything felt strange, weird. The familiar was suddenly unfamiliar. My mother was dying! What does that even mean? I'd always taken it for granted that she was a fixture in my life.

I immediately went to that place where I always go when life becomes unfathomable–behind the mental barrier where I can hide and secretly look out, like a child covering its eyes with its hands and peeking through spread fingers. I went into high gear, becoming super-efficient, filling my minutes with constant activity–agitated depression a counselor once called it–my way of coping.

Mother was in a coma, her entire forehead a solid black and blue mark. We decided to give her food and water only if she requested it. I would ask her if she wanted some, Julie wouldn't and just waited for some indication from her. We each handled it in our own way, neither challenging the other's choice nor setting rules.

There are no rules about death and dying, although so many want to make them. It was a blessing that my family was of one mind. There are often such horror stories about squabbles during a loved one's final days.

My parents' health plan offered us an in-home hospice program which we gratefully accepted. Somehow, dying in your own home seemed right and comforting in a strange way.

Their small two-bedroom apartment became a thoroughfare of coming and going—doctors, nurses, home-care workers and medical equipment suppliers whizzing about, constantly on the march.

My father was overwhelmed by the frenetic pace of it all and just tried to stay out of the way. After being totally engrossed with Mother's care for so long, he barely had a role anymore. He was exhausted and withdrawing more and more into himself, his normal outgoing nature slowly disappearing. It frightened me as I'd always depended so much on his strength.

Dad had been such a take-charge kind of person. Nothing seemed to daunt him. He decided what house we lived in, chose the car we rode in, picked out our vacations, bought the food we ate, and carved the roast at dinner, all the chores of the man of the family. Now, his wife of sixty-one years was the focus of a well-oiled machine that dealt with the business of dying, and he was powerless to do anything.

Mother was neither eating, drinking nor responding. She was in the bedroom lying under the afghan blanket Julie had crocheted.

My son, Richard, and nephew, David, arrived along with David's pregnant wife, Brenda. They had all come into town for the holidays. Was it only last month, after learning that she was to become a great-grandmother for the first time, that Mother had weakly asked Julie if she could hold the baby after it was born?

"Yes." Julie felt compelled to answer, even though she knew Mother would probably not be around to do so.

My mentally challenged daughter, Natalie, arrived from her placement several hours away. Natalie, a child in an adult's body, had always been so needy. Whenever with me, she wanted my complete attention. When Natalie was going to come for a home-visit, I couldn't wait for her to arrive. After about a day, I couldn't wait for her to leave. Mother acted as a buffer, diverting Natalie's attention so I could have a little respite.

Natalie had entered a placement for the developmentally disabled twenty-six years earlier at the age of eight. My then husband, Natalie's father, and I were advised by experts to place her there because we would never be able to teach her properly at home. Up to this point, that was the worst day of my life. Mother's looming death was looking to compete with it.

The whole family had always tried to assemble for the various holiday celebrations. It was actually an official excuse for everyone to get together.

Julie and I each made different dishes for the dinner this time. We decided we'd bring the food over to my parents' apartment and celebrate there. That way Mother would be a part of it in some fashion.

We all sat crowded around the dining room table while Mother remained in her bed, one room away. Natalie was confused.

"Why is grandma sleeping?" she wanted to know.

Natalie always asked the hard questions. I just wanted to avoid thinking about it, but she wouldn't let me. I knew that, like a child, she would just ask again and again until she got an answer–no subtleties with Natalie. How do you explain to an innocent that her grandmother is dying? How do you even explain death to her? How do you explain it to yourself?

"Grandma is going to die, darling," I fumbled badly. "She's going to go away to another place."

"Where's Grandma going?"

"It's a special place. We'll never see her again, but we'll always remember her and talk about her and love her, and she'll always love us."

That seemed to satisfy Natalie for the moment. But, I knew there would be more questions to come. Over the years it has evolved into her simple game.

"Where's Gramma?" she periodically queries.

I bite: "Where's Gramma?" I parrot back, setting up the game.

"Gramma died, Gramma died, Gramma died," she chants in her singsong manner, repeating the words like an advertising jingle, neither of us comprehending their meaning. Yet the game has been completed in its ritualistic way. That's all that matters to her.

What matters to me? Just to get through the damned, obligatory discussion so we can move on to something else.

"One day at a time," I whisper to myself, as the recovering alcoholics say. I think we're all recovering from something.

While we were eating, someone at the table would occasionally stand up and walk into the bedroom to spend time with Mother. No one had decided on that in advance; no one questioned it; it just happened that way. We made up the rules as we went along. It was the only thing we could do when nothing made sense.

At the end of the dinner, we went into the bedroom together and stood around the bed. Mother looked so tiny under that beautiful afghan. Each of us took turns saying something to her. I saw her hand move slightly under the cover. Was it just a dying reflex? Did she hear us? I choose to think it was the latter.

Two days later my mother died.

The boys and Brenda had left town the day before. Natalie was still home, waiting for me to take her to the airport that day to fly back to her placement. She traveled as an unaccompanied minor, watched over by a flight attendant even though she was an adult. The airline used to accommodate me in that manner, although it wasn't official.

Natalie and I rushed over to my parents' apartment. Dad was dazed but efficient–my mentor in how to handle emotions. He took Natalie to the couch in the living room to distract her while I went into the bedroom to be with Mother. She looked stiff and strange–sort of frozen. I sat down and just stared at her. Where was I? Where was my body? Was I breathing?

I was looking at a replica of my mother. I touched her face–it was so cold. I'd always heard that dead bodies are cold–it's true. How could my mother be cold? I didn't understand. I just sat there, numb. I couldn't cry; I couldn't move; I couldn't feel. All I could do was stare at her.

After a while, I don't know how long, Julie came in and said the man had arrived from UCLA to take Mother's body away. Several years earlier, my parents had both willed their bodies to the University of California at Los Angeles for medical research in order to pay something back to the world and help humanity.

When they had first mentioned it so long ago, I thought it was bizarre and repulsive. I didn't want to talk about it. The thought of over-eager medical students cutting up the bodies of my parents was horrible. The alternatives weren't much better: sticking their bodies into a box and burying them in the ground or burning them up.

They would periodically bring the subject up, slowly, gently, aware of how hard it was for Julie and me to accept. I finally agreed to discuss it with them, realizing that they needed to do this. On a certain level, I respected them for taking charge of their own deaths—practical to the end as was their way.

The body mover—is that what you call him, does he have a job title?—removed Mother's watch and handed it to Julie. He asked about her wedding ring and I said it wouldn't come off as her knuckles had become enlarged and misshapen with arthritis. He assured us he could remove it and did so easily, with Vaseline I guess. He handed the thin gold band to me. I stood there looking at it.

Julie mentioned that it had been her original wedding ring. Many years earlier she gave it to Mother to use when Mother's knuckles became too swollen for her own ring. I offered it to Julie. She declined, saying she had no need for it as she now had another one.

I didn't have any pockets in my pants and didn't know what to do with the ring, so I just slipped it on the fourth finger of my right hand. It's been about eleven years now and it's still there. Every time I think about removing it, I always decide to put it off and think about it another time. Although I hardly even realize it's there anymore, in some strange way it keeps Mother with me.   Maybe I'll remove it someday.

Body Man asked us to leave the room while he put Mother's body on a gurney.

Get your damn hands off my mother! I wanted to shout, but didn't.

Everything was surreal. I was walking and talking, but on automatic.

Natalie was sitting on the living room couch wearing the large headphones my father used to hear the television better. She was giggling and rocking back and forth to whatever was playing on the TV.

"I having a fun time, Mommy," she said when she saw me.

As I had walked into the hallway between the two rooms, I was positioned for an instant at a point where I could see into both the living room and the bedroom at the same time. I was caught in a bizarre nightmare. I could see Natalie in one room rocking on the couch, and Body Man in the other room doing something with Mother. One eye was looking at life in its pure exuberance and the other was spying on death in its finality. That momentary image remains with me along with Mother's wedding ring. I don't think I'll ever remove either one of them.

I dreaded having to tell Natalie. I walked back into the living room where she was still stationed in front of the television set. She looked so adorable in those oversized headphones that I started to cry.

"What the matter, Mommy?" she said with alarm.

Natalie has always been keenly aware of my moods and becomes very upset if she perceives the slightest, negative emotion on my part. I hugged her.

"You upset, Mommy? You mad at me?"

"No, darling, I'm not mad at you. I love you," I said, trying to make my voice sound normal, but not doing a good job of it.

Awkwardly, I started to explain her grandmother's death to her. Although I tried to simplify everything, it all sounded ridiculous, like a gruesome bedtime story.

* * *

"We'll have it in four parts: we'll read excerpts from her autobiography; we'll show a video of her life in photographs; we'll have eulogies; and we'll say a prayer."

Julie and I had been planning a memorial tribute to Mother almost from the day she died. It occupied us and let us channel our horror into something loving and giving. It also kept us together in our grief as we fussed over each detail.

It would be at my house. Richard would be the Master of Ceremonies. We would invite about fifty people. We'd get platters of food, and Julie and her husband, Barry, would also make some of the dishes.

Mother had taken a class many years earlier on how to write her autobiography. She'd worked on it diligently, asking her brothers and sisters for input. Often, when I would call her and say, "Hi Mom, what are you doing?" she'd answer, "Working on my autobiography."

It sort of became the family joke, but we loved that she was doing it. The autobiography slowly grew, like the afghans my sister loved to crochet, covering her as she worked.

When it was finished, Mother gave a copy only to Julie and me. She said she didn't want anyone else, including my father, to read it until after she died. When I first read the manuscript, it was like being given permission to peer into her most hidden life.

The story started at the earliest age she could remember, that of a young child. Many of the facts and anecdotes she wrote about those times came from her older siblings as she was too young to remember them.

Mother's parents were Russian immigrants with limited money and resources, but not children. Her mother died in 1919 in the influenza pandemic of that time—Mother was only five. The family struggled along with the older siblings parenting the younger ones while their father worked. His earnings were meager and the mouths to feed, many. When he remarried, his wife brought her children into the household forcing their limited funds to stretch even further.

Life for my mother, one of the middle children of that bunch, was always hard. Her stepmother was indifferent to her and her siblings, overtly favoring her own children. She was a poorly-educated immigrant, the same as her new husband, and life had always been a struggle for her, too. Mother never got over the deprivation of her childhood, and it colored her whole life.

The autobiography continued through Mother's young adult years, her young married years, her motherhood years and her grandmotherhood years. Some of the revelations made me sad, and I wanted to hold and comfort her. I felt contrite that I hadn't done so as she declined rather than arguing with her and trying to get her to be reasonable. How unimportant "being reasonable" seemed now that she was gone.

Dad had also come from a family of Russian immigrant parents. Although money was more plentiful than in Mother's family, emotional attention was not. His father was cold, preoccupied and dismissive of his only son. My father never spoke of that, simply commenting that "he was a hard man" when I once asked him about his relationship with his father who had died when I was very young.

Dad at Age 2

Charismatic with outsiders, Dad was hard to live with. He could easily become enraged, and he saved his temper for his wife and daughters. Although not physically abusive, his emotional swings could be terrifying.

Being the oldest child by five years, I challenged Dad's authority first when I became a teenager. During our arguments, Dad's voice would become louder and louder.

"This is my house and if you don't like it, just get the hell out," he'd scream.

Mother tried to intervene, but he shouted her down, too. Julie would hide behind one of the stuffed chairs in the living room while Dad stormed on, afraid that she'd also become his target if he noticed her. Although definitely intimidated, I would hang in there before eventually backing down. The backing down got less and less as I got older and older.

I think Dad subconsciously admired me for refusing to submit to his bullying, maybe because he hadn't been able to do so with his own father. Being the victim himself of that oppressive behavior, I eventually understood that Dad was emulating the only role model he knew. "Typical," as psychologists might say.

I don't know why I had the guts to confront Dad and risk his wrath. Maybe I was just getting sick of his domineering and tyrannical ways. Those were the seeds of rebelliousness that grew ever so slowly and painfully over the coming decades against those who have tried to manipulate or control me.

Somehow, I have managed to put Dad's rages behind me. Julie, on the other hand, has never gotten over her anger at his treatment of her when she was a child. To his credit, Dad did try his best as he aged to atone for his behavior. However, it was only in his later years, as he mellowed and Julie and I matured, that we were all actually able to enjoy being with each other.

Dad had never read Mother's autobiography. Now he would see it. I was concerned about his reaction as it contained some hurtful things about him.

Mother detailed the early years of their marriage when they had moved from Chicago to Los Angeles during World War II, because Dad was able to get a job in the flourishing aircraft industry. The move was difficult for Mother, being away from her family and alone in a strange city with a young child.

Mother had written from her heart. Her marriage was not gratifying. Dad was wrapped up in himself and she didn't get much emotional support from him. This would be difficult for Dad to learn, although I knew that on some level he was aware of it.

Julie and I chose significant passages from the autobiography to read at the memorial service. We decided to each alternate and tried to include information about many of the family members who would be attending.

Dad and Mother in Their Courting Years

Barry took charge of having a video made of relevant pictures. We gathered one night at their house to pour over suitcases full of old photos, trying to distill them down into manageable piles. We followed the outline of the autobiography, separating the photographs by age and epoch.

We picked out beautiful music to be included with the video as it was playing. We wrote a statement at the end explaining about Mother donating her body to UCLA. When the video was finished and returned to us, it was just what we wanted.

Richard found an appropriate prayer on the Internet. Others wrote eulogies.

On the day of the memorial, everything went as we had planned. We had roses throughout the house reminiscent of Mother's name. On one small table, I placed a solitary rose in a bud vase next to a lone candle.

As we did while she was dying, we made up the rules as we went along—our rules. We all agreed that we wanted to decide for ourselves how to pay homage to Mother. It made it more personal, more ours.

I spent a long time in private writing my eulogy. It began:

"My mother's name was Rose, and that described her perfectly. She was beautiful and glorious, but sometimes she could be prickly and thorny. Yet, she was always very special."

I could see Dad weeping softly as I read, keeping his head down so others wouldn't see him. It unnerved me to watch my father so beaten down.

CHAPTER 3
The Invitation that Changed Our Lives

"Come with me to my acting class, Daddy," I said.

I had recently retired from my career of thirty-seven years as a probation officer. It was a strange career for me. I had led a sheltered life while growing up, certainly never interacting with anyone who had broken the law. Throughout my career I dealt with people who had committed crimes ranging from minor offenses to some of the most reviled acts in our society. I discovered that they were fragile human beings just like me, but had chosen coping mechanisms that were illegal and sometimes even heinous.

There was a heroin addict who told me that although he had been clean for a long time, he purposely returned to drug use because he was so worried he'd "fall off the wagon." It was just easier than living with the anxiety of possible failure. I didn't understand what he meant.

"Let's put it this way. When you go into a restaurant, you don't even think about it; you just feel like you fit in. When I go into a restaurant, I know

I'm not like the other people there. If they knew what I'd done, they'd shun me. I don't fit into regular society."

At Work as a Probation Officer

Maybe I was drawn to being a probation officer because it allowed me to peek through a keyhole into the hidden parts of life and look beyond peoples' affectations. It helped me realize that I wasn't the only imperfect one. On the surface, most hide their blemishes and only present a happy, contrived face to the world. It's easy to believe that you're the only one with faults and inadequacies—life's little secrets that we all carry and are afraid to reveal for fear of being hated or ostracized.

Is everyone secure and confident but me? I'd ask myself on very rare occasions.

I may look confident in my high school graduation photo, but I'm not.

After all, I was usually spending a tremendous amount of time and energy on presenting to a judgmental world my own version of a happy and successful person. That didn't allow much time for being brutally honest and confronting my own unhappiness and insecurity.

I had never had any thoughts nor aspirations of becoming involved in acting. As a matter of fact, I really didn't care much for actors. In my brief encounters with some of them, I found many to be rather self-absorbed.

Once, many years earlier, I was invited to a party where the majority of the other guests turned out to be actors. As soon as they found out that I wasn't an actor, most I spoke to quickly got bored and moved on to someone else. The only thing they seemed interested in discussing was acting. I decided never again to have anything to do with actors.

Shortly before I retired, I met a woman, Celeste, at a large dinner party I attended. She was seated next to me and we struck up a conversation.

"I'll be retiring in a few months," I mentioned, "and I'm not sure what I'm going to do with myself."

"I have a suggestion. I belong to a group called The Nine O'clock Players through the Assistance League of Southern California. We put on children's plays in our own playhouse. Why don't you come as my guest and see if you like it?"

Well, why not? What do I have to lose?

I attended the performance and was highly impressed by their professionalism. It actually looked like the actors were having a wonderful time. I wasn't really interested in doing anything involving children–raising my own was enough. But, that was the first germ of an idea I had about getting involved in any pursuit connected to acting.

After I retired, I started exploring things I might do in my new and uncomfortable free time. I'd always been so active and totally occupied that a calendar full of reading, going out to lunch with friends and taking long walks was just not stimulating enough. I experimented with attending a few lectures and doing some volunteer work, trying to find a niche for myself in this next phase of my life.

My longtime girlfriend, Diana, told me about classes offered through Santa Monica College at an affiliated, senior program called Emeritus College. A few weeks later, as I was leisurely thumbing through their catalogue, I noticed the Theater Arts section. I remembered how much fun the performers seemed to be having at that children's play I had attended.

I saw a scene-study class listed and simply assumed the protocol was that the students sat in their seats and took turns reading aloud from a play. It sounded interesting enough and was only once a week. I figured I could handle that, so I decided to enroll.

I entered the classroom for my first session and immediately felt intimidated. It was obvious that almost everyone else had been attending for quite a while and knew each other.

Partway through the class, one of the students walked over to me, handed me a scene from a script and asked me if I'd like to read it with him.

"Sure," I responded, taking the script without much thought.

He walked up to the head of the classroom, turned around and gestured to me.

"Come on."

"Where?" I answered, becoming anxious.

"Come up to the front of the class," he replied, a bit irritated since I hadn't moved.

Oh my God! We stand in front of the class and read?

That wasn't what I had expected. My old nemesis, stage fright, reached up and grabbed my throat.

Throughout my career, I had dealt with murderers, robbers, rapists, etc, the most frightening and dangerous people in society, but I had never conquered my fear of speaking in front of a group. I always felt naked and vulnerable. It probably stemmed from childhood when we had to give book reports while standing in front of the class. The other students would snicker and whisper among themselves, finding any fault they could with the poor kid stumbling over his speech.

I briefly thought of bolting. Instead, I meekly got up from my seat and slowly walked toward the front of the class, dragging it out as long as possible. I kept trying to calm my nerves. After all, I was a mature adult—a senior. This stage fright wasn't going to get the best of me. As I turned around to face the class, I became aware that a sea of eyes was focused on me. I was ten years old all over again and it was book report time.

Oh, help!

I looked at the papers in my trembling hand and saw that it was the opening scene from *Death of a Salesman*. If I'm going to start, I'm going to start at the top, right? My mouth was dry and my tongue seemed to be stuck to the roof of it.

How do I get out of this?

As I started reading the part of the wife, Linda Loman, in what seemed to be someone else's voice, a totally unexpected thing happened. I became so engrossed in the character and the scene that I completely forgot that a roomful of strangers was critically assessing everything I did, and maybe snickering and whispering.

When we finished, I looked up and everyone was applauding. I felt as though I were being physically lifted up by the group and carried on their shoulders. What a high. I was hooked!

My scene partner was very excited at how well the reading had gone. He asked if I'd be willing to perform it with him in the class showcase.

"What's a showcase?"

"We rehearse during the semester and then perform our scene onstage in front of an audience. We do it with props, costumes and blocking."

"What?" I mumbled, my old friend stage fright making me choke on the word.

My old friend had lived inside of me for too many years to simply slink off into the night. However, out of my mouth came the words, "I guess so."

That was the beginning of my metamorphosis. I was set on a journey to break free of the ball and chain of stage fright that I hated so much and had dragged around for so many years.

* * *

"No, I don't think so," protested my father softly.

Dad had seemed so lost since Mother died. He was trying to act normal, but an uncharacteristic quietness engulfed him. I was worried that without Mother, he'd feel that life just wasn't worth living.

"Oh, come on. You'll love the acting class."

Dad was naturally outgoing and full of himself. He loved to tell jokes and was so captivating that he held his listeners spellbound. I remember that when I reached the age of fifty-five, I was eligible for my first, senior citizen discount at a hotel. I was so excited that I told everyone about it.

When Dad heard, he joked, "Do you know how you can tell when you're getting old? When your daughter gets a senior citizen discount."

That was Dad—even his jokes had him as the main attraction.

It had taken me years to figure out that Dad was actually an insecure person, always having to prove himself to the world. How old do you have to be before you give yourself permission to analyze your parents and admit the truth that you find?

I had also become aware that my parents each married the right person. Mother was naturally quiet, soft spoken and introverted. Dad was loud, the life of the party and a total extrovert—always "on." He brought interest and excitement to Mother's life, and she brought peace and calm to his. They certainly could get on each other's nerves though; too much of a good thing can get old after a while. However, over the years they had adapted to each other.

Mother, Julie and I had learned from Dad's sisters, Aunt Sandra and Aunt Doreen, that when he was young, his father always demeaned him, never having much use for his oldest child and only son who was not the "jock" he had wanted. As a consequence, Dad had outdone himself to succeed in the areas his father would have admired: saving money and never having to rely on others.

Dad at Age 8, with His Sister

The down side was that much of his behavior was unconsciously geared to bringing attention to himself–filling that bottomless well. It used to irritate my mother, and as she aged, she was no longer willing to tolerate Dad's grandstanding.

Dad had controlled Mother for years, always besting her because he could yell louder and was in charge of the purse strings. Now, it was her turn. Oh, how they did their dance, as most long-term partners do.

Mother slowly turned from mouse to lion. We started calling her "The Mouse that Roared." She'd confront Dad every time he started trying to impress everyone. It would make him angry, but it worked. He'd knock off the blustering and skulk off, subdued for the moment.

And why couldn't I confront Dad like Mother had–everything always having to be about him, sucking all the air out of the room as they say? Because, if I had, it would have been tearing him down. How could I tear down the man I saw as a God–the source of my strength? The truth, of course, was that over the years our positions had switched. He now leaned on me. However, in my mind, nothing had changed.

The closest I had ever come to a serious confrontation was when Dad was already an old man. I don't even remember what he had said to his grown grandsons, but I felt it was way too controlling and overbearing. I told him that I wouldn't be a bit surprised if they told him to, "Go fuck yourself."

He became very quiet and slowly looked up at me.

"How could you talk to me like that?" he said so stunned, as though I had hit him.

I was devastated. I apologized all over the place. I felt horrible.

Mother and Dad had each changed in subtle ways. It's funny how life often brings us what we need without our knowing it. As he aged, Dad no longer had the strength to maintain his posturing. Being "on" all the time was too exhausting. Mother pricking his balloon was his official excuse to back down.

Dad and Mother in Their Senior Years

Conversely, tired of always being in the background, Mother had amplified her voice as Dad's became more muted. She challenged his position on center stage, thereby elevating her own importance and protecting him all at once.

One of the special experiences that comes to mind about that era of their marriage started shortly after Dad retired. He quickly become bored and found a part-time job as a secretary to a company vice president. After working three days a week for several months, his boss told him she now needed a full-time secretary.

"Rose, why don't we each work for her part-time in the one job?" Dad suggested to Mother.

Mother had been a secretary before their marriage and she liked the idea. The two of them worked out a proposition and presented it to the boss. They would each work different days of the week in that one position, thereby fulfilling the job of a full-time secretary. The boss agreed to give it a try.

It was really pretty efficient. They would plan at home what the other needed to do the next day on the job. If one couldn't go in on his/her assigned day, the other would substitute. The boss never knew who would show up, but it didn't really matter. Their one position got a vacation and other company benefits. It was a neat experience for them both which went on for two or three years until they decided to retire.

Slowly, as the years passed, Dad mellowed and morphed into a loving, caring husband, father and grandfather. He became much more solicitous of Mother, helping her walk instead of walking ahead, and asking her what she wanted to do rather than just deciding by himself.

By the time she was failing in her final months, Dad had become Mother's caretaker. It was very difficult; she could be cranky, griped constantly and was more bitter than ever. Dad bore it with dignity and rarely complained. He had gained a lot of insight into himself and their relationship. He felt he wanted to make up for being so self-centered and unavailable to Mother's needs in their early years together. Well, he certainly succeeded. Now he was lonely and had no purpose.

* * *

"You can just sit in the back of the classroom and not say a word if you don't want to. Just give it a try."

"Okay, if you really want me to."

Dad didn't have the energy to keep resisting me. I knew he'd love it and I thought it might help him cope with my mother's death.

Friday came, I picked up Dad and off we drove to acting class. We walked in and took some seats toward the back. Dad was quiet and I could see he felt awkward. We sat among the others who were all knowledgeable about acting.

The teacher, Barbara Gannen, was a petite brunette in her fifties with an outsized personality dressed in upscale funky. When she finished taking attendance, she started calling students up to the front of the class to participate in an improvisational, acting exercise. By the mid-point of the class, several teams had already completed their scenarios.

"Marvin, you're going to be a judge and Ruth will be a defendant pleading her case in front of you," Barbara said casually, pointing to Dad.

Before I could even turn to see how he was feeling about it, Dad was on his feet walking jauntily to the front of the room. A bit reserved at first, he started off slowly. In no time at all, he warmed up and was obviously loving it. As a matter of fact, we needed a hook to get him off. A thespian was born!

I had always envied Dad's ability to command an audience without a second thought–no stage fright for him. It's strange how insecurity can manifest itself in diametrically opposed behavior: never calling attention to oneself versus constantly calling attention to oneself. I was getting pretty sick of the "never" and wanted to get in on some of the "constantly."

Dad was an immediate hit with the class, but that didn't surprise me; he was in his element. Instantly, he had a roomful of new, best friends. As a father and daughter in the same senior acting class, we became the sideshow oddity, wonderful to possess and shout about.

On the way home, Dad couldn't stop talking about it. He felt that he had been one of the best performers. He wouldn't let me leave without agreeing to pick him up for the next class. Throughout the following week, he called me repeatedly to discuss it. The class had become number one on his dance card—his new passion.

Dad and I started discussing acting all the time. He was also discussing it with anyone else who would listen. His grandsons were patient with him and got a big kick out of it at first. After a while, though, it started getting tedious. Dad had a way of grabbing onto something that attracted him and not letting go no matter what happened.

Athletics was a perfect example. During the time I was growing up, Dad had never been interested in sports. However, as his two grandsons grew older and became avid sports fans, he started following sports in the newspaper and watching games on television. I remember him checking the TV Guide and writing all the sporting events he wanted to watch in his calendar.

Richard and David were especially fond of the Lakers basketball team, so Dad watched each of their games faithfully. He would talk about Shaquille O'Neal as though he knew him personally. I guess every Lakers' fan does the same, but Dad had a way of saying it so that you'd wonder for a moment if he really did.

"Hi, Dad. What are you doing?" I'd typically ask when I called him.

Often the reply was a version of: "Oh, I can't talk now, I'm watching the game." Lately, "the game" was always on.

Who was this man? He sounded a lot like my father, but something was fishy. Now Dad was a sports aficionado? When Dad got his claw into something, there was no dissuading him. As usual, he assumed everyone else thought it was the greatest thing in the world, too. When Dad liked something, he loved it!

Dad became totally engrossed in the acting class. When we walked in, he'd make his way up ahead of me to sit in the front row and was anxious to be called upon immediately. That's Dad. Everything becomes an extreme; it's either horrible or wonderful.

After careful observation of our class members, I had come to the conclusion that acting classes tend to attract big personality types. Almost everyone wants to be top banana–one-upping the other. Even casual conversations during class breaks were same. Each one was vying for the floor to "wow" the next one with clever remarks, anecdotes and tales of his achievements. Well, that certainly described Dad. That type of larger-than-life personality is very easily deflated, however. Hurt feelings periodically broke out.

Barbara had her work cut out for her: how to get the best effort from everyone, make it fun and interesting, and not drive people away in a huff of anger. I saw it happen more than once. One time, a class member suddenly, without seeming provocation, stood up, started complaining loudly about being passed over for his perceived turn to read his scene, and stomped out, never to return.

Dad had the potential for just such behavior as I'd seen down through the years. He had usually sought out social situations where he was the main attraction. His friends were most likely to be low-keyed types who just loved it when he dazzled them with his charm and personality. When he had a rival, there could be an explosion.

I remember when we went to a party for out-of-town relatives hosted at a cousin's house. Dad wanted to make a comment during the speech being given by one of the guests of honor, who, also an attention-grabbing type, kept cutting Dad off. After several attempts to break in, Dad turned red in the face and exploded loudly with "I want a turn to speak."

The two of them got into a tiff, right in front of everyone at the party. After the speech went on awhile longer, the floor was yielded and Dad got the chance to make his comment. It turned out to be some inane remark, not worth all the hullabaloo. In my ongoing quest never to call negative attention to myself, I was thoroughly embarrassed since it was my father behaving like a fool.

At the acting class, we were in a roomful of "Dads." He might not like the competition.

After a few sessions, Barbara told us to bring in some scenes from plays which we would read in class with a partner. She'd help us decide on the best one and then we would start rehearsing in order to perform it in the class showcase. Just the mention of that word started butterflies doing the jitterbug in my stomach. Not Dad–he was ecstatic; he'd show them all a thing or two.

Dad no longer drove a car. A few years earlier, he had begun to have occasional "mini-strokes" as the doctor called them. There was no medication and no cure. One would come on suddenly, last about a minute or two and be gone just as fast.

When one of those incidents occurred without warning, Dad would suddenly freeze in place, his speech would start slurring, he'd become unsteady on his feet, and he'd be unable to engage in conversation nor do much of anything until it passed. It was frightening to watch and could be dangerous if it happened when he wasn't in a safe environment.

Mother had asked me to tell Dad that he couldn't drive a car anymore; it was just too dangerous. I was the one who could "talk to your father" as Mother used to say when she wanted something and knew he'd resist vehemently. Julie, too, would come to me as a conduit to Dad. For some reason, he usually listened to me.

We'd go out to lunch and I'd bring up the matter in question at an appropriate moment. Dad would give me that look and then laugh, knowing that Mother or Julie had put me up to it. He'd bitch and moan for a while, but would finally give in after I presented my reasonable bullet points. It was my family's own version of triangulation.

Having to give up driving is a crushing blow to anyone–a real loss of independence. Dad grieved the loss of driving for a short time, but in his characteristic way, he soon adapted. In no time at all, he was riding the bus to the doctor for his medical appointments and walking to local markets. He didn't let much get him down for too long.

I was careful never to mention his car. It sat in the garage for about two years, as he secretly had hopes that he'd be able to drive again. One day, without prior discussion, he called me.

"I've decided to sell my car. Put an ad in the newspaper, will you?"

It was amazing the good ideas Dad came up with sometimes. Often, the best thing to do is just let things gel. It was much better that he had made his own decision, or at least thought he had.

Because of Dad's inability to drive, Julie or I had to drive him places which were so far away that walking or going by bus wasn't an option. Acting class was one of those.

Since the students pair up to do scenes and spend a lot of time outside of class getting together to rehearse, a potential scene partner for Dad would always have to come to his apartment for their rehearsals, and never the other way around. I imagined that most people wouldn't like that. The only reasonable solution was for Dad and me to be partners. However, I had already committed myself to the other classmate to perform in *Death of a Salesman* and also had a second possible partner for another short scene. I could barely handle those, but now I was faced with being in three scenes when I'd never even done one.

What a mess!

Well, I had no choice. I couldn't back out of my original promises, yet I couldn't let Dad down, either. I'd just have to do all three. This acting business was getting to be a major pain!

I soon realized that I had a big problem. I didn't know of any plays with a role for an eighty-five year old man except *The Sunshine Boys*. We couldn't do that one, though, since it had already been performed at a recent, class showcase before we joined. I didn't want to tell Dad and spoil his enthusiasm. This was a real dilemma.

I knew that a couple of class members had written and performed their own material. One had been a professional comedy writer before retiring. The other just seemed to have a natural gift for writing. Although the teacher discouraged original writing by class members, she did occasionally allow it with her approval.

I wondered if I could try to write something for Dad and me, and maybe for my possible third scene. For the final years of my job, I had compiled data on criminal defendants and written reports to assist judges in passing sentence. I had learned how to express myself in written form, distilling a large amount of material into a concise report. But, that writing had been technical and investigative in nature. I had never done any creative writing before. Well, I didn't have much choice; I figured I'd give it a try.

CHAPTER 4
Our First Scene:
"Going to the Movies with Dad"

What would I write about for Dad and myself? My mind had been tinkering with a few incidents.

On my first day of acting class, which was held in a typical classroom with rows of seats parallel to the blackboard in front, I had sat in the almost full, second row. The first row was empty except for one seat occupied on the end by a very large man. Halfway through the class, he got up and walked out, returning about five minutes later. However, instead of taking the seat that he had only recently warmed, he sat down directly ahead of me, instantly blocking out my view of the entire teacher and about a third of the blackboard.

I tried in vain to see over his shoulder. I moved my chair a few inches to either side as room would allow, but that didn't work as there was just too much of him. I was totally hemmed in. I just sat there staring at the man's back. I felt like a small child at a parade–boxed in and unable to see the action.

Something similar happened again a few weeks later at a crowded movie theater. Before the film started, a huge man walked in and sat in the only seat available, which was two seats directly in front of me, blocking about a quarter of the screen. I groaned simultaneously with the average-size man sitting just ahead of me. Throughout most of the movie, every time Huge Man moved his body to one side, Average Man and I moved our bodies to the opposite side. Since I was in the back row next to the left wall, I finally sat up on my armrest and was instantly about a foot higher. It was exceedingly uncomfortable–a one bun job, but at least I could see.

Those two incidents kept playing themselves out in my head. Something about them was intriguing, but there was still an element missing.

As Dad had aged, more and more he reminded me of "The Nearsighted Mr. Magoo," a character in a movie, cartoon series when I was a child. The movies back then always showed a portion of a "serial" (to be continued next week–hooks you into coming back) and two full length movies with "the cartoons" shown in between.

Mr. Magoo was a stereotypical curmudgeon, so nearsighted that he could barely see anything. A crotchety, irascible little old man, he went around town getting himself into the most outrageous situations. Since he couldn't see what was happening, he would completely misinterpret everything, walking off grumbling about it. Everyone who came into contact with Mr. Magoo was always baffled by his antics. Did the creator of Mr. Magoo know my father? I also had this in the back of my mind as I was thinking about writing our scene.

About a week later, I woke up in the morning with the whole concept of *Going to the Movies with Dad* in my head. Without my knowing it, Mr. Magoo and the two "big man" incidents had converged in my subconscious.

First, I made handwritten notes. Then, I sat down at my computer and typed out the scene, inserting stage directions. This took some trial and error as it was my first stab at it. I used whatever formats I could remember from reading plays and invented some of my own along the way. In the process, new angles of presenting things emerged and I was able to tie everything together.

I realized that much of the material was simply based on an exaggeration of Dad's behavior. He was my inspiration for what I had put down on paper. I had been observing him my whole life, and now it was coming in handy. Sometimes, I would break out laughing as I realized that what I was composing were things he might actually do given the proper circumstances. I was writing a love letter to my father with him as the star. In a few hours, it was finished.

Here is the script:

GOING TO THE MOVIES WITH DAD
By: Lee Gale Gruen

(An elderly man and his daughter are walking down
the aisle into a movie theater.)

Daughter
This is so exciting, Dad. We haven't
been to the movies together in ages.

Dad
It's so dark in here. I can't
see anything.

Daughter
Your eyes will get used to it soon, Dad.

Dad
There are so many people in here.

Daughter
Just watch your step. You'll be okay.

Dad
Why is it so noisy?

Daughter
Don't think about it.

Dad
What movie did you
say this is again?

Daughter
Oh, it's that new Tom Cruise movie.
Everybody is talking about it and
I've been dying to see it.

Dad
Tom Cruise, who's that? I thought
it was with Clark Gable.

Daughter
(exasperated)
No, Dad, he's dead.

Dad
WHAT? Gable dead! When
did that happen?

Daughter
(pause)
Let's just look for a seat.

Dad
I can never see in the movies,
because I always end up sitting
behind some big moose.

Daughter
I know, Dad, and I've thought
of the perfect solution. We'll
find seats behind one empty seat.
Nobody ever sits alone, so you'll be
able to see everything. LOOK,
there's one. Let's get it quick. It's so
crowded in here, it's probably
the only one.

(Dad and Daughter make their way into the row and Dad sits behind the empty seat.)

Dad
Did you bring my back rest?

Daughter
Yes, Dad. Here it is.

Dad
The trouble with movies
today is there's too much cussing.
When Clark Gable used the
first cuss word in a movie, we
were all shocked. We finally got
used to it, but the movies
today have no respect for
common decency.

Daughter
(rubbing forehead as if
getting a headache…..then,
trying to divert Dad's attention)
Look, Dad, here's your popcorn
and coke. And, I brought your
favorite snacks.

Daughter
(shows Dad the snacks, pulling
them out of a bag one at a time)
Milk Duds and Crackerjacks and…

Dad
(interrupting her)
How far is it to the bathroom?

Daughter
(in an exasperated manner, trying
to placate him)
It's just outside the door.

(Suddenly a very large man begins to walk down the aisle. When he is near their row, Daughter notices him. She does a double take and her eyes open wide, incredulous. The man begins to make his way into the row just ahead of Dad and Daughter. Daughter is following him with her gaze, moving her head to

65

watch him. Slowly, her mouth drops open as the man takes the seat in front of Dad.)

Daughter
(brief pause…..shouts)
OH, SHIT!!!!!

(Daughter throws all the snacks up into the air in pure exasperation)

* * *

A few days later, I picked Dad up to go to acting class. He was all ready, decked out in a sport jacket and tweed, golf-style cap. This was the highlight of his week and he wasn't going to go about it casually. I handed him a copy of the new script, worried if he'd like it. As he was reading, he'd laugh periodically.

"This is great," he said when he had finished. "But, who are we going to get to play the moose?"

"I thought I'd ask Irwin."

He was the large man who had sat in front of me in the classroom on my first day. I had told Dad about that incident.

"Perfect," said Dad. "But, do you think he'll do it?"

"We'll see," I answered, certain that he would. After all, there was no reason he wouldn't; the part was innocuous enough.

When we arrived at class, I approached Irwin and handed him the script.

"Would you play the part of the moose? It's only a short, walk-on part with no lines."

"I'll read it and let you know."

Later, when I went back to discuss it with him, he was highly insulted. He angrily handed me back the script and huffed, "this is a fat man's joke." Oh, that artistic personality again.

I was shocked. I hadn't meant to hurt him. Actually, I hadn't even thought of him as fat, only big.

"I never used the word 'fat' in the script. I only spoke of a very large man. That doesn't mean fat. A person can be large without being fat. I would never insult anyone that way. I'm very sensitive to that because my sister has been battling obesity for years," I babbled on, trying to explain.

I had run the scene by Julie to make sure it wasn't offensive. She simply laughed and showed no other reaction.

I guess I said the magic words, because Irwin begrudgingly relented and agreed to play the part. I thanked him profusely, appropriately humble. The truth is that he was the only one in class suitable for the role, and without him it wouldn't have been nearly as funny. I learned a lesson: begging and cajoling are part of show business.

We all went up to the front of the class: Dad, Irwin and I, to do our first reading of *Going to the Movies with Dad*. Would the teacher like it? Would the class like it? Just like my first reading of *Death of a Salesman* in front of the class, this would be the maiden voyage of my writing. I was jittery.

During our reading, I heard laughter coming from the room. When we finished, everyone applauded. Well, I was hooked all over again. Just give me those applause, baby.

I might have written the words, but Dad's delivery had the right "tude." Because of his attitude along with his natural presence, he could carry it off. Yes, it's all in the delivery!

Dad was beaming. He had suddenly become the big man on campus. Everyone was making a fuss over him. He couldn't get enough. Just give him those applause, baby. I really was a chip off the old block.

We rehearsed both in and out of class. I'd often call Dad on my cell phone when I was driving and we'd run our lines. Thank God for cell phones.

Whenever I could, I'd go over to Dad's apartment to practice. I'd rearrange the furniture to approximate the stage. Then, Dad and I would go through our lines and do the blocking a few times until he became too weary to continue. I always had to be careful of the pace because of his growing frailty. That regularly hindered our progress, even though the excitement of the rehearsal usually carried him for a while. Little by little, we got better. Dad was fairly good at remembering his lines, but some were a problem. I made him palm-size, flash cards—senior cheat-sheets—to hold in his hand. They had key words to stimulate his memory—ah, the eighty-five year old brain.

Dad never could remember Irwin's name and kept referring to him as "the moose." We'd giggle about it and I'd always tell him, "Irwin, it's Irwin, Dad." I'm sure Dad refused to learn his name because it was so much fun laughing together—one more link in our bonding.

As we progressed, Dad's personality shone through into his character and he would slightly edit what I had written. For example, one line was: "What, Clark Gable dead, when did that happen?" Dad began playing it as: "What, Gable dead, when did that happen?" banging his cane hard and indignantly on the floor—his idea—on the opening word. I was irritated.

"Dad, use his first name, too."

But, Dad was stubborn and kept playing it his way, as though by using only Clark Gable's last name, he had a professional relationship with him. That was Dad. He'd insinuate himself into a situation and raise his own importance.

Once, Dad had owned a few shares of Viacom stock. When it split, the company kept offering larger and larger pay-outs to its thousands of shareholders, big and small. Dad was definitely among the small. Nevertheless, he talked about it ad nauseam as though the company were courting him personally. Each time he found a new prey to tell his Viacom story to, I'd mentally roll my eyes. I had never even heard of Viacom before and I grew to hate the very word.

Well, of course, Dad was right. Somehow, the elimination of Clark Gable's first name personalized it, which is how a lot of people think of their relationship to movie stars. It's funny how the addition or subtraction of one word can make such a difference. Doesn't that happen in everyday life all the time? I've often thought that since verbal communication is so difficult, we might be much better off if we simply stopped talking altogether.

Dad came up with another idea for how he wanted to play his role. At the end, when the moose sits in front of him and Dad can't see, he would stand up and peer first over one of the moose's shoulders and then the other, trying to get a glimpse of the movie screen. From the audience's point of view, all they would see was Dad's head over the moose's shoulder. It was actually very funny. Dad then planned to look at Daughter and frown. That would be the impetus to send her over the edge after having been so patient with his complaining.

Dad kept practicing his frown on me wherever we were. Again, we'd burst out laughing every time he'd grimace. He really was a riot.

Each week, Dad and I continued to present our scene in front of the class and we always got laughs. Class members began to take him under their wing, sort of adopting him. One man, the former comedy writer, was completely captivated by Dad. He'd laugh and laugh, the ultimate compliment. He loved Dad and loved my writing. Let me tell you, that's very easy to take.

Even though everyone fawned over Dad, he always made it a point of telling them that I had written the script. He would often confide in me that he felt bad because my part was the straight man, and that I ought to write funnier lines for myself. He failed to realize that the lines were only half of it; his personality and delivery were the other half.

Our large props were three folding chairs, two side-by-side and another one in front of them, representing the rows of seats in a movie theater. Our smaller props were a pillow for Dad's backrest; a shopping bag containing a box of Milk Duds candy and a box of Crackerjacks; a bag of popcorn; and a large, paper cup with a Coca Cola label on it.

I painstakingly gathered the props. With no problem, I found a box of Milk Duds being sold at a movie theater. However, Crackerjacks were another matter. I finally googled the word "Crackerjacks" to find the manufacturer's telephone number and called to find out where I could buy them. Sure enough, they were sold at a local supermarket. Although I only wanted one, I had to buy a three-box group all glued together, but hey, expense is of no concern for the sake of one's art, right?

Several weeks later, I went to the movies with my friend, Beverly. I didn't want to buy a large bag of popcorn nor a cup of Coca Cola, so at the end of the movie I started scouring the theater aisles and trash cans, enlisting Beverly and a few ushers to help. Eureka! We found an empty popcorn bag—ditto for a large cup labeled Coca Cola. But, hey, dumpster diving for the cause is a no-brainer, right?

Armed with our props, Dad and I were invincible. Everything in the scene came together. We were a success! Our classmates loved us! But, what would a live, critical audience think?

CHAPTER 5
Performing Onstage in the Class Showcase... What a High!

It was the day of the showcase. I had barely slept the night before and was a wreck. I tried to compose myself, but my head was going in every direction. Dad and I had invited just about everyone we knew. My mind was doing a number on me.

What if we forget our lines? What if we trip and fall? What if I drop the props? What if, what if, what if? Stop that, I scolded myself.

It was no use. I had three scenes to do. What if I said lines from one scene in the other?

I had heard that Arthur Miller, the playwright of *Death of a Salesman*, who was still alive then, was very particular that every production of his famous play be performed just as he wrote it. I imagined him hearing about me delivering the wrong lines and filing a lawsuit.

Me (on the stand): "Oh please, Arthur, I didn't mean it. You see, I'm crazy, and I committed to being in three scenes when I've never even acted before in my life. What do you mean, you don't care? Now just a darn minute, Arthur, that's pretty heartless. No wonder Marilyn divorced you!"

When I finished gathering all the props and loading them into my car, I drove off toward Dad's. I actually arrived in one piece. I have no idea how I got there. As usual, Dad was waiting on the sidewalk in front of his apartment, dapper as ever.

"Hi, Dad. How are you doing?"

"Oh, fine honey."

He was calm and collected. He got into my car and we drove off. The theater was in the basement of the Santa Monica library. Being affiliated with the City of Santa Monica, our class was allowed to use it. We were running lines as we drove. It's miraculous the effect that has on me. I calm down immediately when I'm portraying a character other than myself. Human emotions are so interesting. I've heard that people who stutter can become actors because they stutter only in their real lives, not when they're playing another person.

About a half hour later, we arrived at the theater and I parked the car. I noticed several class members driving in and parking, also. Everyone was waving to each other. It was like a small town. We all shared a common experience and the rest of the world was composed of outsiders—us versus them.

Dad and I started unloading our props. Actually, I was doing the unloading; Dad was doing the talking-to-everyone-else. We knew our places and each did it well.

Dad and I walked into the theater. We had rehearsed there a few days earlier and knew just where to go. However, today was different. Today was going to be the big time. It's quite overwhelming to be on an empty stage in a theater looking at the seats an audience will soon fill. We were awestruck.

All the other class members were carrying in their props. Nervous chatter and activity were interspersed with setting up the prop tables. In our very low-budget production, card tables doubled for prop tables.

The props for each scene are arranged on a separate table so when it's time for that scene to be set up, they are organized and immediately available. Each acting partnership was responsible for arranging its own prop table. Of course, in a large theatrical production there is a prop master. We all doubled as prop masters, stage hands and just about everything else.

Dad and I were learning acting terminology. One of the other actors mentioned going onstage through "the hole in the curtain." I was incredulous. I had never known that there were holes in stage curtains for actors to go through. When I weakly asked him for an explanation, he looked at me as though I were a complete idiot.

"You know, the hole in the curtain."

That's what I like, using a term to define the same term! Well, I quickly gave up on that. Anyway, we were all very high strung and irritable. He probably hadn't slept well the night before either.

I subsequently learned that the hole in the curtain is the terminology for the middle split between the two halves of the curtain. God, I was green. Did I hide it well enough? Probably not.

We learned more terminology. Upstage means the part of the stage behind the action, furthest from the audience. Downstage is the opposite of upstage. Stage right means the side of the stage to the actor's right as he faces the audience, and stage left is the opposite of stage right. I still find those terms confusing and must visualize myself standing onstage before I can say them correctly.

Actors were everywhere, changing into their costumes or running lines in every available place. They were in the wings, behind the back curtain, in the bathroom, and outside of the stage door. When actors run lines, they go into their own mental space no matter where they are physically. Their concentration is so great that they often have no idea what is going on around them. It's quite something to watch. All was now controlled chaos.

Barbara arrived a short time later and took charge. She seemed to be everywhere at once. Some of the more experienced actors were her designated helpers. They would be operating the electric control that opened and closed the curtain, directing the scene changes, notifying the actors how much longer before their scene, and a million other little details.

With Dad and Our Teacher, Barbara Gannen, Backstage at the Acting Class Showcase

The excitement was growing. It was getting close to show time and the audience began arriving. I peeked out from the side of the curtain and saw some of the people Dad and I had invited walking down the aisle and taking seats. It just made me more nervous.

I started doing some low-impact aerobics to calm down. I have found that I can't sit still when I'm backstage waiting for my scene. I'm in constant motion. Others just sit quietly in chairs. I've never been able to figure out how they do that. I have to keep moving. It's the only thing that calms my nerves.

Barbara gathered us together for a final pep talk. It went something like:

"Well, this is it. You've been working very hard all semester. You're all fabulous (show biz speak for: you don't totally suck) and well prepared. Remember to just go out there and have fun."

Then, she walked through the hole in the curtain—see, I can talk the talk—and we could all hear her welcoming the audience. Barbara was explaining that we were a group of actors from the Emeritus College Acting Class and would be performing various, short scenes. She gave a brief introduction to the first act, setting up the pre-story scenario for what the audience was about to see.

With that, we heard the mechanical sound of the curtain parting to reveal the stage setting for the first scene. The production was launched!

Everything was a blur of activity. I was trying to stay focused. I checked the posted scene-order notice that Barbara had taped up on the wall. My serious scene from *Death of a Salesman* was to be number seven in the lineup, a wait of over an hour. My scene with Dad was number eleven, the last on the program. My third scene, a short simple comedy I also wrote, was number two on the program. I would have preferred to get them all over with sooner rather than later. Then, I could have relaxed.

Oh well, nothing I can do about it.

I started running lines with my *Death of a Salesman* scene partner. I helped other actors move their props on and off the performance area. I ran lines with Dad as well as with my third partner. I couldn't eat a thing—too anxious. I was sure I'd lose five pounds by the end of the day.

My first scene went off very well, but was not really complicated. *Death of a Salesman* would be a real challenge. Finally, Barbara was in front of the curtain giving our pre-scene introduction. I hurried to my mark on the stage and the curtain was drawn.

I was dressed in a long robe—my own comfy turquoise chenille—low budget, remember? I was at home waiting for my husband, Willie Loman, to arrive from a sales trip.

I remembered everything as I became immersed in my character. I went through the blocking just as we had rehearsed it. I couldn't even see the audience members because of the bright, stage lights which pointed toward the actors. It didn't matter, I had forgotten about them anyway. I was totally into the scene. It has given me a great deal of confidence to know that is how I react when I'm onstage. My auto-pilot kicks in and I forget about everything else.

When the scene ended, I heard a roar as the curtain closed. It was the audience clapping. That snapped me back to reality. It took a moment to make the transition. The applause was like a wave washing over me.

Oh, there was an audience out there? Oh, I'm not really Linda Loman?

I can certainly understand why people become actors or politicians or the like. It's empowering!

Dad greeted me as I came offstage. He congratulated me; he had been watching from the wings. I reverted to a little girl, basking in my father's approval. Enough of that, my work wasn't done; I couldn't rest yet.

It was getting close to my scene with Dad and he wanted to run our lines again. First, I had to change out of my "Linda Loman" robe and into my clothes for our scene. I did so quickly, having worn much of my "Daughter" outfit under the robe. Dad and I sat in the semi-darkness of the backstage area— kept that way so the light wouldn't show under the bottom of the curtain behind the ongoing scene. We ran our lines in a whisper so as not to interfere with the scene playing out onstage. Most of the other actors were doing the same.

Occasionally, I'd check the posted notice to figure out how many scenes were still remaining before it was our turn. It was getting very close now. Other actors in their stagehand personas began moving our prop table into place. The current scene ended and the curtain was drawn.

As our props were set up, Dad and I took our positions in the wings, waiting to make our entrance. I glanced at him for one final check. He was composed. I had my props in my hand. He had his cane, ripe for banging. We were quiet, listening as Barbara announced our scene. The control operator pushed the button and the heavy curtain slowly began to part. As if in a dream, Dad and I walked onto the stage, now transformed into the movie theater of our scene.

Everything went exactly right. Dad banged the floor with his cane, precisely on cue. The moose was perfectly moose-like, and Daughter totally lost it at the end. Then, we heard the sound of thunderous applause.

The audience was ecstatic! Was it louder than for any other scene? It seemed that way. As we walked off, I was certain I could see some people on their feet. It was probably our friends and family members, but I didn't care. A standing ovation is a standing ovation.

The curtain closed and a semester of work was over in five minutes. But, the high lasted a week– better than drugs, a lot cheaper and legal!

The entire cast lined up quickly for the curtain call. As the curtain opened, the audience was clapping. We bowed and then gestured toward Barbara in the wings as we'd rehearsed.

She walked onstage and someone handed her a bouquet of flowers. One of the class members owned a florist shop, so they were free. But, hey, it certainly looked classy. Barbara bowed and thanked everyone, including the audience.

The stage was quickly stampeded by audience members coming to congratulate the actors. Our friends surrounded us. They couldn't stop talking about how wonderful we were. Everyone was laughing and euphoric. Dad was basking in it all and so was I. The whole thing was totally upbeat. We introduced everyone around and then to Barbara and several other class members as they happened by. No one wanted to leave.

As everything slowly wound down, people began to drift away. Dad and I, with the help of my friends, Alice and Mark, gathered up our props and started carrying them to my car, still critiquing the performance. That was all anyone wanted to talk about. Dad and I couldn't get enough.

Now, it was time to leave our enchanted world. We drove back to Dad's apartment. I was completely drained. Dad, as usual, was quite composed–doesn't anything fluster that man? But, it was obvious that he was thrilled. Our entire conversation was about the performance. Everything else paled in comparison.

I dropped Dad off and headed for home. I was so exhausted that all I wanted to do was sleep. Well, forget that, I was too wired. There was no way I was going to be able to fall asleep.

I called Richard to tell him how it had gone. He had been following our progress in our regular telephone calls. He was as excited as Dad and I were.

* * *

Dad was crazy about his grandchildren. When I was growing up, Dad's insecurity and need to present a perfect face to the world gave him little tolerance for his children's misbehavior, especially if he felt that it reflected poorly on him. However, that had receded, and when he became a grandfather, he turned into the flip side of the coin. Now, he was loving and giving toward all of his grandchildren.

Dad, and Mother when she was alive, were both especially gentle and caring toward Natalie. They helped me tremendously to cope with having a mentally challenged child. That's not what I had planned for my life. I was supposed to have a husband, two bright and adorable children, a house with a white picket fence, a dog–the whole package.

Being a mother was quite difficult for me. Maybe it was because one of my children was handicapped. Such a child can take over your whole life. I felt overwhelmed, especially after my divorce from their father.

In truth, I had always hated housework and domesticity and loved school and my job. So, I hired a baby-sitter and returned to work to keep my sanity. It was a constant struggle juggling my job, time with my children, and time just for myself.

Natalie's handicap did not become apparent until she was about three years old. She was still not talking at that age and communicated by grunts and gestures. I was worried, but would console myself with the knowledge that Albert Einstein did not talk until he was three. Maybe Natalie was a genius.

At the playground, other mothers could sit on benches and socialize while their children played on the equipment. I had to stand right next to Natalie, because she'd often fall off the swing or slide.

Having a child like Natalie stripped away that defense I had so carefully crafted over the years to convince myself and everyone else how perfect I was. Her strange and offensive behavior brought all the unwanted, negative attention I detested so much, scattering onto me by extension. There were so many incidents that pain me to remember.

I can't even count the times I took Natalie shopping or to a restaurant and she threw a tantrum, screeching at the top of her lungs. With a normal child, you can reason with them, threaten a punishment, or offer a reward. None of that worked with her. People would gather in a circle around us, staring and tsk-tsking. Some would offer their unsolicited advice. I couldn't think straight. I wanted to run away. I wanted to dig that proverbial hole, crawl in and disappear.

I remember the time Natalie and I were invited to a birthday party for the precocious, twin girls her age who lived across the street. During the party, everyone was in the backyard when I became aware of a commotion at the swing set. Natalie was trying to crawl onto a chair swing which had room for four children, and the twins were pushing her off. One said, "we don't want you." Natalie simply walked off and didn't seem to pay any further attention to it. However, I felt as though I had been physically assaulted–like I was the one who had been rejected. The rest of the party was ruined for me, and we left early with me offering some lame excuse.

A handicapped child is so demanding that its normal siblings can be significantly deprived of parental attention. I knew Richard had need of me, too. I tried very hard to be available for him. I became a Little League soccer mom, bringing oranges for a snack to the team of twelve-year olds when they practiced. I attended most of his games, cheering him on when he performed well and bolstering him up when he didn't.

When Richard was a teenager, I encouraged him to join a neighborhood youth group. When he refused to even check it out, I called one of the adult leaders and she arranged to have one of the girls in the group call and invite him. He never knew I was behind her invitation. He loved the group as it filled a void in his life and softened the pain of that difficult age.

I was subconsciously resentful toward Natalie and racked with guilt for feeling that way. It was a long time before I accepted that I must protect my visibly imperfect child from a cruel world—to love her for what she was instead of hating her for what she wasn't. I was forced to ask myself what was more important, my child or what others thought of me. That was a hard lesson to learn and is still ongoing.

Accepting Natalie remains a challenge to this day. Her behavior in public is strange, off-putting and embarrassing. There continue to be so many incidents where people stare at us, many with aversion.

There was that party only a few years ago at a friend's house. She invited me to bring Natalie who was on a home visit. While at the party, Natalie, in her gentle way, kept trying to approach an adorable little eight year old girl and talk to her. The child, with a look of fear on her face, kept backing away into her mother's waiting arms. The mother, a visual carbon copy of the child, put her arms protectively around her daughter and the two of them, now molded into a single statue, glared at Natalie in horror. Of course, by that time all conversation had stopped and everyone was staring at the bizarre floor show. I kept trying to divert Natalie's attention, but she was obsessed with wanting to connect with the child. My head was throbbing and everything became surreal.

Not only is the odd-acting person ostracized by others, so is her family. Even now, I have an internal struggle when my old insecurity buttons are pushed by Natalie's behavior in public. Those early seeds that are planted in us have a way of hanging around forever, exerting their influence and control well into our old age. Nevertheless, I keep on doing battle against myself in behalf of my vulnerable daughter.

My childhood, teen years and early adult years were fully controlled by what others thought of me. I have to credit Dad with teaching me that. When I was growing up, it was so important in his life how he was being judged.

I think Natalie helped both Dad and me to become better people, to throw off the mantle of being so overly preoccupied with how we were being perceived. I am convinced that I would not have the confidence I have today if I had not had my handicapped daughter in my life.

Dad with His Grandson

As much as he loved her, it was difficult for Dad to have a lot of contact with Natalie who lived a significant distance away. On the other hand, his two grandsons lived locally and he spent as much time with them as he could. He counseled them as they grew up and taught them whatever it is that grandfathers teach their grandsons. He was there for them whenever they needed his help, advice or just emotional support.

Richard wore his hair quite long while he was a student at the University of California at Berkeley, as was the style at the time. His usual outfit was cut-off shorts, a sweat shirt and sandals.

Shortly after graduation, Richard secured a prestigious internship at a major organization. Taking it very seriously, he announced to me that he would have to cut his hair (my prayers had been answered) and buy some business suits (in spades).

"Make an appointment for me at Pedro's Barber Shop for when I come home, will you, Mom?"

Pedro was the barber who had first cut Richard's hair when he was about a year old. He was still in business at the same location more than twenty years later.

"Okay, honey," I responded nonchalantly. *Yeeeaaah*, I thought privately.

Dad, upon hearing about it all, was so proud.

"I'll take him shopping for some business suits, shirts and ties."

The momentous day arrived and Richard was dressed in his usual Berkeley attire. Off we went to the barber shop. Pedro was thrilled to be the chosen Delilah to Richard's Sampson. The walls of the shop were filled with photographs of his clients down through the years. Many were children.

I brought my camera for the historic event. To Richard's annoyance, I snapped photographs of the entire process. In about an hour, my typical college son had become a respectable businessman, at least from the neck up. Dad arrived, and he and Richard drove off. Later that evening, they returned to the house and Richard disappeared into his bedroom before I even saw him. In a short while, he appeared in the kitchen where I was preparing dinner.

I turned around and beheld a stranger. My son, only hours ago a boy, had grown up right before my eyes. He was dressed in a three-piece suit with all the trimmings including his new short, conservative haircut. The transformation was shocking. I suddenly felt very old. How could this sophisticated man be my son?

Dad was beaming and so delighted to be part of kicking off the next stage of Richard's life. Naturally, part of the attention splashed onto Dad, as usual. If there was attention to be had, he would figure out how to get in on the pickings.

* * *

"Mom, this is so neat," I heard Richard saying over the telephone. "Why don't you write a whole series of Dad and Daughter scenes? You could call it *Adventures with Dad.*"

"Oh, no, Honey," I protested, but my head started working.

What an interesting idea.

My mind played with it over the next several days. I knew I'd have to come up with a new scene for Dad and myself for the coming semester. The first one was such a success. Maybe Richard had something there. Thus, the germ was planted, and *Adventures with Dad* began brewing.

It soon became apparent that Dad and I weren't finished performing our maiden scene. Dad had a good friend, Chuck, who always invited us to his large family picnic each summer. Dad had called him and told him about our scene. Well, of course, Chuck insisted that we perform it at the picnic in a few months. That's all Dad needed to hear.

"Chuck wants us to do our scene at his family picnic. So, we'll have to start rehearsing it again. When can you come over?"

That was Dad. When he was enthusiastic about something, he simply assumed that everyone else was, too. It never occurred to him that I might not want to do it or might even have other plans. But, of course, he was right; of course, I wanted to do it.

When Picnic Day came, we needed someone to play the moose. I found the largest man there and asked him to do it. He loved the idea.

"But, what's my motivation?" he said after reading the script.

It was surprising how everyone who got involved with this project always had such a good time. All the people at the picnic loved our performance and applauded loudly. Again, they were our friends, but we gladly accepted any adoration without questioning the motives.

I was a regular, weekly hiker in the Santa Monica Mountains with a particular hiking group from the Sierra Club. Some of the hikers had come to our showcase.

One day, I received a phone call from my friend, Roxie. She was planning a party to honor the hike leaders of our group. Would Dad and I consider performing our scene at the party? Would we! Boy, this was escalating.

Again we needed a moose. By this time, I was experienced at recruiting. I walked up to the largest man at the party, a total stranger to me, and asked him to play the role. He was a gentle giant and graciously accepted. As we performed, he really seemed to enjoy participating. Once again, we were a big success. Once again, the experience was totally positive for all involved, performers and audience alike.

A few months later, Dad and I flew up to visit Richard and David. We had decided to perform our scene at Richard's apartment for them and other family members who lived there. I packed all of our props for the flight–they folded up well and didn't take up much space in my suitcase.

With Dad and My Nephew Performing
"Going to the Movies with Dad"

We needed a moose one more time. David is 6'3" tall and large-boned. He would make a perfect moose. As we performed the scene, he was giggling throughout most of it, a little embarrassed, yet having a great time.

Summer was winding down, and the new semester was fast approaching. I still hadn't thought of a new scene.

CHAPTER 6
Our Second Scene:
"Going Camping with Dad"

Throughout the semester break, Dad kept asking what I was going to write for us next. I hadn't actually written anything yet, but the idea of something to do with camping kept playing in my mind. I'm not sure why; maybe it was the sporting goods store I had gone to the month before. It just seemed like such a ludicrous idea to take a frail, eighty-five year old man camping. Of course, Daughter, with all her good intentions, would be clueless.

It was almost time for the new semester to begin. Dad, predictably, had been reminding me for days. On the morning of the first class, he called me to remind me one final time, in case I had forgotten. With Dad, there's no chance of forgetting anything that's important to him.

"No, Dad. I haven't forgotten. I'll pick you up in front of your apartment at 10:30 am."

I knew he'd be waiting there at 10:00, just in case.

I arrived at his apartment and there he was, sitting on a retaining wall, looking spiffy. Was it my imagination or was he just a bit more stooped over than a few months earlier?

It's probably just my imagination, I thought, as I brushed that idea from my mind.

Dad got into the car slowly with the help of his cane in one hand while he held onto the door frame with the other. He had a little trouble with the seat belt, so I helped him. After all, those seat belts can be tricky. Off we drove to class with Dad chattering the whole way.

"Have you had any ideas about what you're going to write for us this time?" he casually mentioned for the hundredth time.

"Ah, I've been toying with an idea, Dad. But it's not fully developed yet."

"Well, I'm raring to go!"

We finally arrived at the class and I let Dad off in front while I went to park the car. I didn't want him to have to walk too far as I knew it would tire him out. That had become our modus operandi: after I dropped him off, Dad would wait on the sidewalk in front of the building until I got there, and we'd saunter into the classroom, arm in arm. Although my holding his free arm was a gesture of closeness, it was also my way of providing additional support for him without making it obvious. He never acknowledged it, but I'm sure he knew.

As we entered the classroom, we were greeted with applause from the other students.

"There he is, the star of the show," said Barbara, with a dramatic sweep of her arm and an abundance of enthusiasm.

She caught us unaware and Dad blushed a little.

"No, everyone was great."

Although Dad craved attention and basked in it when he got it, there was a generous quality to him. He did, most of the time, remember to share it with others. No one in the class seemed upset that Barbara had made that remark. Dad was the oldest member of the class and everyone doted upon him. He didn't seem to be a threat to anyone, and he was so endearing in whatever he did that everyone just wanted to make him special. That was okay with Dad. He had been waiting for this niche all his life and he'd finally found it.

At the first meeting of a new class, Barbara always asks if anyone has brought in a scene to work on. That is the embryonic stage of our process. Choosing an appropriate scene is quite difficult. We are encouraged to scour plays to try to find a two-person scene that has conflict, interest, and can be adapted to senior actors. If Barbara approves the scene, she will work on it to cut unnecessary material, possibly knit together two separate passages, change the characters, or do whatever is necessary to make it right for our class.

It's a fascinating procedure. I have seen comedies turned into dramas, male roles turned into female roles, and all other types of innovations. Since we don't earn money on these performances, it doesn't infringe on any copyright of the core material.

A few teams with scenes read them and we all listened to Barbara's critiques. When the class was over, Dad and I left. The original process was now reversed. He waited near the curb while I got the car and drove it from where I had parked to where he was waiting.

Then, he entered the car, again using his cane and the doorframe for support. What an efficient operation we were.

Driving home, I could tell that Dad was tired. He never complained, but when he stopped talking, I knew he was out of energy. I'm so much like him. I'm not comfortable with silences, either. When they come, I instantly fill the space with words. But, just like my father, when I'm tired, that compulsion melts away.

The next day, when Dad was refreshed once again, he called. He wanted to know how I was coming along with the scene.

"I'm working on it, Dad. I'm definitely going to make it a theme about camping."

The camping idea, which had been germinating for a long time, was starting to take root.

"Fine. Get it over to me as soon as you can."

I sat down at my computer and started typing, just letting whatever was going to happen, happen. I don't know exactly where the ideas came from, but come they did. I threw in everything from my own camping experiences, that of friends, some I could envision Dad doing, and some I just made up.

Slowly, a story began to emerge. My creative process has been very interesting for me to observe. Just letting my mind wander seems to be the key. Ideas gradually spring to consciousness that I didn't even know I had. The only way I can explain it is that thoughts and observations enter my mind, mix themselves up there subconsciously somehow and regurgitate in another form. Is it that way for all writers?

After an exhausting few hours, I had written the basic skeleton of our next scene. Now, it just needed a title.

I thought of staying in the same vein as our first scene. If this was going to be a series, it would seem appropriate for the titles to have a theme. So, *Going to the Movies with Dad* now became *Going Camping with Dad.*

I worked on the scene over the next several days, honing and polishing it. Finally it was finished.

Here is the script:

GOING CAMPING WITH DAD
By: Lee Gale Gruen

(An elderly man and his daughter have just entered their campsite. Daughter is carrying an armful of camping gear. She throws it down, stretches her arms up and breathes deeply.)

Daughter
Isn't this exciting Dad? We
can commune with nature.

Dad
(slapping his neck)
Ow, something bit me!

Daughter
Oh, don't worry Dad, I
have some bug spray.

(Daughter searches through the camping gear, finds a can of bug spray and sprays it on Dad.)

Dad
(sneezes and begins wheezing)
I think I'm allergic to that
bug spray. Quick, get my inhalator!

Daughter
(searches through the camping gear)
Here it is, Dad.

(Daughter hands inhalator to Dad, who begins inhaling it deeply while Daughter stands by looking concerned. Then, she returns to sorting out the camping gear.)

Dad
Where's the bathroom?

Daughter
(is involved with sorting camping gear and points toward end of stage)
Over there, Dad.

Dad
(looks to where Daughter is pointing)
Where?

Daughter
(again points to same place)
Over there.

Dad
(confused...looking around)
Where?

Daughter
Over there, behind that boulder.

Dad
(looking puzzled, walks to boulder)
There's nothing here but a
hole in the ground.

Daughter
(still distracted with sorting camping gear)
That's it!

Dad
(looks perplexed)
How do I go to the bathroom
in a hole in the ground?

Daughter
Oh, just squat.

(Dad looks down at hole while wobbling on his cane and practicing trying to squat, looking very bewildered. Dad returns to Daughter, who has just spread out two sleeping bags on the ground.)

Dad
Where are we going to sleep?

Daughter
(points to sleeping bags)
There.

Dad
Where's the bed?

Daughter
We're sleeping on the ground.

Dad
Are you crazy?

Daughter
That's what the Native Americans did;
that's what Early Man did.

Dad
(huffy)
Well, I'm not a Native American
and I am definitely Late Man.

Daughter
(trying to distract Dad)
Look Dad, here's a fishing pole.
I saw some guys over by the
pier and they're willing to take you
with them on their boat.

Dad
The only fish I've ever caught
were in a goldfish bowl.

Daughter
(hands Dad the fishing
pole and leads him offstage)
Go ahead. You'll have fun.

(Daughter returns to sorting camping gear. Lights
dim. Lights come up and Dad re-enters looking
bedraggled and carrying broken fishing pole.)

Daughter
(horrified)
DAD!!! What happened?

Dad
Well, first I got into the boat and
skinned my knee on the oar.
Next, I tried to put bait on the
hook and cut my finger. Then,
I threw in the fishing line and
fell into the water after it.

Daughter
(incredulous)
Just forget about it, Dad. Look, it's starting
to get late. Let's roast some marshmallows.

(Daughter hands Dad a stick with a marshmallow on the end.)

Daughter
(points offstage)
Hold it over the campfire that I
made right there, Dad.

(Dad walks offstage to roast marshmallow.)

Daughter
(pause...yells)
How's it going, Dad?

Dad
I don't know, it's too
dark to see anything.

(Crashing sound and swearing is heard offstage.)

(Dad walks back onstage with face blackened, hat scorched and holding a stick with a burnt marshmallow on the end.)

Daughter
(staring at Dad in total dismay...it's the last straw)
Oh, Shit!!!

(Daughter drops all the camping gear she is holding)

* * *

The next day I called Dad and told him I had finished the script.

"Come right over," he ordered.

Once a manager, always a manager.

"I have some things to do, Dad, but I'll be over as soon as I can."

"Okay, but hurry."

Two hours later, I was at Dad's apartment. He opened the door and stuck his arm out.

"Let's see it."

No further words were necessary for Dad at this point. He knew what he wanted and let's get to it.

I handed him the script. He carried it over to the couch, sat down and put on his glasses. I watched anxiously. A big smile gradually took over his face. Occasional laughter accentuated it. Finally, he put down the script.

"This is great…really funny. But, how am I going to do all those costume and makeup changes?"

"I'm sure one of the other cast members will help you, Dad. You'll have your own personal dresser."

Dad really liked that idea. He was moving up in the acting world–his own personal dresser.

The day of class arrived and so did Dad and I, script in hand. Dad didn't even wait for the teacher to call on us.

"Barbara, we have a scene to read," he shouted from the back of the room as we walked in.

Everyone turned toward us with anticipation. Barbara, used to the impatience of the elderly, laughed and said, "Great, Marvin. Come on up now and do it."

We walked to the front of the class and started to read. I heard chuckling coming from the room. When we had finished, everyone was clapping and shouting kudos. Actually, they were so in love with Dad that he could have read the encyclopedia and they would have roared. Barbara was laughing, too, and said it would be perfect for the showcase. Dad was thrilled!

As the weeks went by, we eased into our rehearsing routine. It was much easier this time because we were used to it and things came automatically.

I started thinking about props again. We'd need lots of camping gear. Where was I going to get it? I began asking friends and class members. I called Julie.

"Do you have any camping equipment that I could borrow for our scene?"

"Come over and look in the garage," she suggested. "I don't know what Barry has in there."

Julie and Barry had been going to garage sales for years and buying every conceivable bargain, whether they needed it or not. They had a treasure trove of anything one might need for any purpose.

The next day the three of us convened in their garage. Soon, there was a pile of camping gear in the driveway. I plowed through it and chose two sleeping bags, a Coleman lantern and a fishing pole.

I needed the marshmallow props. I found Styrofoam balls in a craft store which were perfect. But, what would I put them on? I needed something sturdy that Dad could easily carry–a twig, of course!

In my backyard was a huge apricot tree that grew from a seed I had planted. Year after year it had remained as barren of apricots as a bald man's pate.

"Okay, honey," I said to the tree (now I'm talking to a tree?) "It's time to make something of yourself."

I stripped two straight twigs of their leaves and wedged the Styrofoam balls on the ends, wrapping one with black electrical tape to simulate the burnt marshmallow. A few old pots and pans along with a red and white checkered tablecloth and a picnic basket filled the rest of my prop requirements. We were ready to roll.

I met with Dad and began dividing the props equally between us. Well, I really was the clueless daughter. Maybe my character was actually based on myself. Dad had one hand totally devoted to using his cane. Also, he couldn't carry anything too heavy or cumbersome as he was somewhat unsteady on his feet even with the cane.

We both looked at the Coleman lantern at the same time. It was compact, not too heavy and had a long handle on the top–perfect for Dad's one free hand. That left all the other props for me. I hooked some over my shoulders, put some under my arms and had several in my hands. Picking them up had to be choreographed in a certain sequence in order to fit harmoniously on my body. It was a major production in itself.

Now I understand why the more experienced class members use only a minimum of props, I huffed under my breath.

The semester progressed as all the class members partnered up, chose scenes and began to perform them in class. It got to the point where I practically had most of the other scenes memorized, too. We all watched each other's progress. Soon, everyone was off-book (had the lines memorized).

It is so much easier to perform when you're off-book. You don't have to keep stressing-out about not being able to remember what you're supposed to say. I was so proud of Dad because he was off-book like everyone else and had learned our complicated blocking, costume changes and prop usage. I was proud of myself, too.

Barbara was always making adjustments and modifications to everyone's performances. No matter how much we had rehearsed or how polished we felt, she could still find something to be improved.

"Tweaky, tweaky," she was fond of saying.

As discouraging as that felt sometimes—won't I ever get it right?—she was the best kind of teacher. She never let us slack off. She really had the uncanny ability to suggest the smallest modification—a pause here, a physicality there, and voilà, the problem you had been grappling with for weeks was solved.

"Even when you're starting to walk onstage to do your scene, I'll still be following you and tweaking," she also liked to say.

Was the woman a drill sergeant in her former life?

It was getting close to the date of the showcase. This time, we were going to perform in a new venue at the Santa Monica College concert hall. It was a much larger theater with a bigger stage meant for musical productions. However, it had wonderful curtains in the front and back of the stage that could be manipulated to make the performance area larger or smaller. We were also going to have our own lighting technician who was an employee of the college. We were moving up.

A few weeks before the showcase, we had a technical rehearsal just for the purpose of planning the lighting. Then, we acted out our scenes in their entirety so that we could get used to the stage and its requirements. The blocking had to be altered in many of the scenes to adapt to the new setting. Everything changes when the venue changes.

The day of the showcase arrived. I was nervous, but certainly not like the first time. Now, I knew what I was doing and what to expect. Dad, as usual, was composed and full of confidence.

Two cast members were assigned to act as Dad's dressers when he went offstage during our scene. At his first exit, one dresser would take the fishing pole from him, dismantle it and hand it back to him. The other would roll up one of his pant legs, turn his baseball cap sideways and pull out one of his shirt tails. When he exited the second time, one would dab black makeup on Dad's face and cap to make it look like he was covered in soot. The other would hand him the twig with the burnt marshmallow on the end.

I also had an additional serious scene with a different partner, just like before. My serious scene was to be first on the program. That was good, I would be able to give my full attention to Dad and our complicated scene. We were to be up fourth.

Dad and I ran our lines several times backstage. Naturally, we were very quiet so as not to disturb the scene onstage. Actually, we just sort of mouthed our words. We felt so professional!

Scene three was just about finished. I handed Dad the Coleman lantern, laughing inwardly because he looked so precious. I outfitted myself with my mountain of props in just the right order. We took our places in the wings, waiting patiently.

After Barbara announced our act, the two parts of the curtain slowly separated and Dad and I walked onstage.

Everything proceeded smoothly. Dad was adorable, as usual, and put his own special twist on his lines and movements. Only I could tell that he was just being himself. We were near the end of our scene. So far, so good. It was time for Dad's character to exit for marshmallow roasting while my character remained onstage.

I was moving around my props according to the script while Dad was in the wings being prepped by his dressers. From where I was onstage, I could see him out of the corner of my eye, ready to come back in his disheveled persona.

After I said my cue line, I watched him in the wings as he began to walk back onstage. Wait! He was holding the twig with the black Styrofoam ball, but his arm was straight at his side with the ball pointing toward the floor.

I'll kill him!

How many times had I told him to hold the stick up so the audience could see the burnt marshmallow? We had rehearsed it over and over. I watched him in what felt like slow motion as he got closer and closer to stepping into the sight of the audience, controlling myself from running into the wings screaming like a maniac about some stupid marshmallow. Ah, the temperament of the creative genius thwarted.

At the last second, just as he cleared the curtain and came into view of the audience, as if it had a mind of its own, his elbow bent, the twig slowly rose and the burnt marshmallow pointed proudly toward the ceiling for all to see. Dad, the old trooper, had come through after all. How could I have doubted him?

Of course, he was a hoot and the audience roared. We exited the stage in a state of euphoria. There was a certain feeling of relief to have it over.

Our props were cleared away from the acting area and the props for the next act were set up.

Just a minute, where's the Coleman lantern?

I realized with dread that the curtain had closed behind it, it was now in full view of the audience and Barbara was announcing the next act. It was going to be onstage during that act, which certainly didn't lend itself to a Coleman lantern. I felt terrible, but I was helpless to do anything. I simply waited miserably until the scene was over and the curtain closed. Then, I ran out in full view of the audience, retrieved that confounded object and made a quick retreat.

**With Dad Onstage Performing
"Going Camping with Dad"**

The showcase ended. The audience was enthusiastic as we all took our bows. Our friends and family surrounded us and made a big fuss. We loved it all!

We drove home almost in silence. We were both exhausted, but especially Dad. We kissed goodbye and he got out of the car. I waited as he walked slowly up the cement path to his apartment. From the back, he looked so little and stooped, leaning so hard on his cane. I turned away. It was hard to watch.

CHAPTER 7
Our Third Scene:
"Going to the Airport with Dad"

"Why don't you and Grandpa and Natalie come for a visit, Mom?" suggested Richard. "When you get here, Debra and I will take care of Natalie and give you a rest."

It sounded like a great idea. We hadn't all been together as a family since my mother died. It would be a handful for me, however. I wondered if I could handle traveling with Natalie and my father together. Both were so needy in their separate ways.

Natalie was like a child. Since living in her placement, she had flown on airplanes frequently when coming for home visits, but always under the supervision of the airline flight attendant. She was able to cooperate with the requirements of traveling as long as she was constantly supervised, more for her own safety than because she caused any problems.

My father was completely lucid and mentally sharp. However, he was quite unsteady on his feet and tired easily.

Can I supervise them both and still navigate the turbulent waters of the airport? I wondered.

Shortly after Natalie had gone into placement years earlier, my marriage to my children's father broke up. I sought counseling as my world had fallen apart. The therapist used a vivid word picture to describe my inability to cope with a controlling husband and a handicapped child.

"They were sucking you dry out of both tits."

I saw myself withering like a balloon as the air is slowly being let out–there was nothing left of me. I've never forgotten that description although it's been decades. Would my being with Dad and Natalie together, both so demanding of my attention, be a mini-replay of that scenario?

On the other hand, I really wanted Natalie and Dad to be able to go. I'd just have to make it work.

I became very enthusiastic about the whole thing. I told Dad about it and he was all for it. He would be able to see all three grandchildren together.

I didn't tell Natalie right away because I knew she would become fixated on it and talk about nothing else, trying to fit our departure date into her limited ability to deal with time concepts. Usually, I don't tell Natalie about special events or even my pending visits until close to the last minute because she nags the staff at her placement, bringing it up constantly. I decided to wait until just a few days before our departure to let her know.

I booked our airplane tickets and tried to plan for every possible contingency. I would fly Natalie in from her placement and she'd sleep at my house that night. The next day, we'd take a taxi to pick up Dad at his apartment and then all go on to the airport. It should be simple.

Dad, who hadn't flown on an airplane in years, began making his plans. He bought a few items of clothing and borrowed a suitcase from Julie. He was pretty jazzed about the whole thing.

The big day came and Natalie arrived on schedule. We had a relaxed day, as relaxed as you can be with Natalie, and got a good night's sleep. The following morning, we got dressed, had breakfast and were all packed when the taxi came to pick us up.

We arrived at Dad's apartment where he was waiting for us out on the curbside with his suitcase. He got in, I helped him buckle up and the driver set off for the airport. Everything proceeded exactly as I had anticipated.

We arrived at the airport and were just about ready to step out of the cab.

"I forgot my cane," Dad said sheepishly.

"What? Oh, no."

I hadn't even noticed. I guess Dad had used the handrail to walk out of his apartment building and had just walked the few steps to the taxi and gotten in without thinking about it.

Well, what was I supposed to do with that? We couldn't go back to his apartment to get the cane. We were at the airport ready to catch a plane. Also, I had

Natalie with me who required so much of my attention and energy. But, Dad had a hard enough time walking very far even with a cane. It would be doubly difficult for him without it. I tried to keep calm—deep breaths. I called Richard on my cell phone.

"Honey, we're going to have to buy Grandpa a cane when we get there. He forgot to take his. I think they sell them at pharmacies."

"Don't worry, Mom. We'll handle it," he said, trying to reassure me.

We all walked into the airport with Dad supporting himself on one of my arms and Natalie holding my other arm so she wouldn't get lost. Help, I needed a Fairy Godmother. Sometimes, things just become too much.

I looked for some seats so I could park everyone and gather my wits about me. I spotted a few across the room. We proceeded slowly toward them, three abreast, arms linked. We looked like a chorus of Greek dancers.

As we sat there, I racked my brain about the cane problem. Then, I got an idea.

"Dad, watch Natalie. I'll be back in a little while."

I wasn't sure who was watching whom. However, since Dad was so competent mentally and had a mouth on him, I figured they'd be safe for a while.

I went in search of the Lost and Found. When I got there, I explained the problem to the clerk at the desk.

"My elderly father left his cane at home, and we're about to catch a plane," I whined hysterically."

Maybe "whined hysterically" is a bit strong, but it was pretty close.

"If you have one here, maybe I could borrow it. I'll return it in a few days when we get back. I'd really appreciate it."

"Wait a moment."

In a few minutes, the clerk, bless his heart, returned with a handful of canes.

"These have been here for months. Pick whichever one you want."

He held them out to me. "You can just keep it."

I chose an adjustable one so I could fit it to Dad's height, thanking my savior profusely. Sometimes, the fates are in your favor and all is right with the world.

I made my way back to Dad and Natalie with prize in hand. Dad's face lit up. I knew he felt bad burdening Richard and me with having to shop for a cane. Also, he seemed to feel much more secure now that he didn't have to wait until we arrived before he could get one.

Dad was happy; Natalie was happy; I was happy. That was just a slight bump in the road and I had weathered it pretty well. Traveling with Natalie and Dad wasn't so bad after all.

Onward we went, plunging further into the mysteries of the airport. We proceeded to the ticket counter, checked in and walked to the metal detector. Natalie and I had no problem; we simply took off our shoes and walked through. Natalie, having flown frequently, knew just what to do.

Dad, who hadn't been on a plane since well before the terrorism attack of 9/11, was unfamiliar with the procedures. As it turned out though, he couldn't even go through the detector because he had a pacemaker. He would have to be hand-searched. Dad followed the TSA agent's instructions, but wasn't too thrilled about being patted down. He kept making jokes to relieve his discomfort, trying to be a good sport.

Natalie, on the other hand, was amazed by the whole hand-search production. I was starting to feel agitated dealing with Dad and the TSA guy, and handling Natalie's incessant questions about what they were doing to Grandpa.

We finished with the metal detector and proceeded to the gate. Dad and Natalie were again holding onto my arms so we wouldn't get separated. We painstakingly inched forward.

We reached our destination following a bathroom stop which was another story in itself. I was still taking deep breaths—remaining calm.

We found seats near our gate and waited for the plane. Soon, we boarded and took off. In just over an hour, we arrived at our destination. Without further incident we retrieved our luggage and found Richard at our previously agreed upon meeting place. Natalie stayed with Richard and his girlfriend, Debra, at their apartment, while Dad and I shared a hotel room. True to his word, Richard and Debra assumed the bulk of Natalie's supervision.

We saw David and Brenda as well as Julie and Barry, who had driven there for the occasion. Other relatives living in the area came to Richard's apartment. Dad and I performed *Going to the Movies with Dad* with David playing the Moose. We had a great time and the visit went quite well.

Our stay ended and it was time to return to Los Angeles. Richard and Debra drove us back to the airport and dropped us off at the curb. We all hugged and kissed one another. It was sad to be leaving, but great to be going back to my own home and some tranquility.

Dad, Natalie and I walked into the airport and checked our bags. After repeating the metal detector bit again, we walked to the secure area. It was cordoned off with only a small opening through which to enter, guarded by an elderly airport agent. I don't know how he got that job; he was probably a volunteer. He seemed to be very impressed with his power and had something obtrusive to say to each person who entered. He reminded me of a retired General who never gets over ordering people around. It's usually not an accident how people end up in their jobs, even volunteer ones.

Natalie and I went through the entrance effortlessly. I was busy helping her with her coat when I heard a ruckus.

"What do you have there? Who told you that you could bring that in here?"

"It's a newspaper I found lying on a chair," I heard Dad explain. "I just picked it up. I'm going to read it."

"You can't bring that in here. Put it down, right away!"

"Wait a minute, just who the hell do you think you're talking to?" Dad screamed at the elderly airport agent, who had been screaming at him.

Dad and the old geezer were about the same age and obviously clones from the same donor. Geezer wouldn't stop screaming orders at Dad. He didn't like it that his authority had been challenged.

Who was it who said, "Absolute power corrupts absolutely?"

"*Uh oh,*" I thought.

I know my father. He had always had a short fuse and could fly off the handle easily. Some years earlier, my parents had come to a Halloween party at my house. The festivities were in full swing when they arrived. Dad was very nervous and wanted to make just the right entrance. He was dressed as Dracula and cleverly holding a plastic champagne glass instead of a trick-or-treat bag. Upon entering the house, he accidentally dropped the glass and it broke. His anger flashed instantly, and he began yelling "damn it" over and over while trying to pick up the plastic pieces. He was totally unaware that everyone had stopped talking and was staring at the little old man having a hissy fit.

Thanks a lot Dad for making a spectacle of yourself at the party I worked so hard to arrange.

With Dad and Mother at My Halloween Party

Why is it that I always have to be the calm reasonable one while others have their outbursts? I was getting pretty weary of that role!

Like a flash flood, Dad's temper tantrums usually appeared and were gone just as fast. This was difficult for me as a child, especially when those outbursts had seemed far more frightening. As an adult I'd learned to weather them, and Dad had also mellowed somewhat, so we both had evolved.

Well, Geezer obviously didn't realize that nobody yells orders at Dad and gets away with it. The gauntlet had been thrown down. Dad and Geezer both became red in the face as a senior screaming match ensued.

Geezer: "Throw that paper away immediately." Commanded with a pointing finger.

Dad: "The hell I will!"

Geezer: "I'm going to call the airport security!"

Dad: "Call whoever the hell you want to. I'll have your job for this, you old fart."

Was this the pot calling the kettle black?

I rushed over to Dad as quickly as I could with Natalie in tow. I grabbed his arm and tried to pull him away.

"Dad, let's just go."

He looked at me as though I were crazy— leave a perfectly good cat fight? He was having none of this leaving stuff. He was right in the thick of things and that's exactly where he was planning to stay. After all, how often does one encounter a perfect storm?

Dad and I were about the same height and weight. I grabbed one of his arms and was trying to pull him away, but he was suddenly as strong as an ox—ah, the power of adrenaline. That frail little old man had turned into Arnold Schwarzenegger.

Since I was about twenty-five years Dad's junior, my strength began to win out and we slowly moved away. However, since I was only pulling Dad by one of his arms, he was able to twist his body around. With his free hand he kept waving his fist at Geezer while continuing to yell additional threats and insults.

"Dad, please, we're going to get arrested."

I don't even think he heard me. He was too pumped up with winning the match of the century. Although I was slowly succeeding in gaining some ground, it was extremely difficult because he was resisting me and Natalie was on my other arm repeating over and over, "Mommy, why is Grandpa yelling?"

I don't believe this is happening. It's just a nightmare. I'll wake up in a minute.

I briefly considered having a meltdown but quickly discarded that option. I was the only responsible adult in our threesome. I couldn't dissolve yet.

None of this took place in a vacuum, of course. We were attracting a lot of attention, and brawny types in TSA uniforms were approaching as though to corral us. I guess we looked like a ridiculous diversion, somehow drawing attention away from a potential terrorist elsewhere in the airport. I expected the handcuffs to be clapped on at any moment.

I succeeded in pulling Dad clear of the secure area, but not without a few more dagger glances from him in the direction from which we'd come.

He was still fired up and wasn't listening to anything I said. He was furious and felt he had been totally justified. Since we were now far away from Geezer, and Dad was still in high gear, he turned his wrath on me.

"He had no right to speak to me like that."

"But, Dad, you can't act that way at the airport. Everyone is very uptight because of the worry about terrorists."

Dad wouldn't give an inch. He was sure he was correct and he was holding his ground. Finally, I said the magic words.

"Dad, think how difficult you made it on me, especially since I have to care for Natalie, also."

Dad immediately lost steam and conceded that was the only thing he had done wrong—not thinking about Natalie and her needs which could have posed a problem. He still wasn't buying my argument that we could have gotten arrested. After all, right is right, right?

Thankfully, we got out of there and onto the plane without anything else happening. Of course, both Dad and Natalie had to relive the event throughout our flight back to Los Angeles. I went to my mental Zen place and began to view it all as possible material for our next acting class. I hadn't thought of anything yet and this really could be funny if looked at in the proper light.

Okay Dad, I'll show you. This will appear in our next scene. This is simply research for my upcoming writing project in the continuing saga of Dad and Daughter.

After we left the airport, we did everything in reverse. We took a taxi to Dad's, dropped him off and proceeded to my house. Natalie slept over that night. The next day she flew back to her placement.

The whole experience at the airport had been so traumatic that I kept replaying it in my head. My thoughts began to take shape over the next few days. I stationed myself in front of my computer and just started to type. Once again, a script emerged. In the same style as the two previous scenes I had written, I entitled it: *Going to the Airport with Dad.*

Here is the script:

GOING TO THE AIRPORT WITH DAD
By: Lee Gale Gruen

(An elderly man and his daughter have just entered the airport terminal. Both are carrying flight bags. Dad is walking with a cane and has on an aviator's cap and jacket.)

Daughter
Yah, this is the right terminal, Dad.
It's so exciting. We're going to
fly on a jumbo jet!

Dad
The last time I was on an airplane,
I was wearing an Army uniform.

Daughter
Oh, everything has changed since
then. You're going to love it. Come over
here, Dad. We have to go through
the security check first.

(Daughter and Dad walk over to a table with a sign on it that says "Airport Security Check Point.")

Daughter
Here we are, Dad. We have to put
our bags on the table.

(Daughter and Dad place their flight bags on the table. Daughter picks up a container from the table and holds it toward Dad.)

Daughter

You have to take everything out of
your pockets and put it into
this container, Dad.

(Dad empties his pockets and puts everything into the container.)

Dad

There's something weird about this.
Keep your eye on my wallet.
I don't like this whole thing.

Daughter

It'll be alright, Dad. Don't worry.

Dad

Why is that guy pointing at me?

Daughter

Oh, that's the security guard.
He's chosen you for a hand-search.

(Dad looks at his hands, first the palms and then the tops, in bewilderment while mouthing the words "hand search.")

Daughter
Here, Dad, give the guard your jacket.

(Dad removes his jacket and hands it to Daughter.)

Dad
I don't like these new-fangled,
airplane rules one bit.

Daughter
Dad, the guard wants you to
take off your belt and shoes.

Dad
WHAT! I never heard of such a
thing just to go on an airplane. There's
something funny going on here.

Daughter
No, Dad, that's just how
things are done now.

Dad
So, now everybody goes on
an airplane without their clothes on?

Don't they have laws
against that kind of thing?

Daughter
No, Dad, they just want to
make sure you're not a terrorist.

(Dad bangs his cane on ground.)

Dad
Well, I'm no terrorist, but if
they don't watch it, I'll give
them something to be terrified about.

Daughter
Be quiet, Dad. If you look
suspicious, they might arrest you.

(Dad begins shaking his cane.)

Dad
Just let them try. I know my rights.
Who do they think they're messing with?

Daughter
Here, Dad, the guard wants
you to hold your arms out like this.

(Daughter places Dad's arms straight out from his sides.)

Dad

Oh, so now they're going to crucify me?

Daughter
(exasperated)
No, Dad, they're just
going to pat you down.

(Suddenly, Dad twists around and holds his cane up in the air as if to hit someone.)

Dad

Hold it just a darn minute, young man.
What do you think you're doing? I don't let
anybody put their hands there except my doctor…
or maybe his cute young nurse.

Daughter
(looking around nervously)
Calm down, Dad.

Dad

Hey, now I know what's going
on here. This is really a hospital,
isn't it? You're trying to get
me to go into the hospital.

Daughter
(stressed)
No, Dad!

(Daughter looks bewildered. She gets nearby
wheelchair and wheels it up to Dad.)

Daughter
We're finished here, Dad. Look,
you can use this wheelchair.

Dad
I knew it! This is a hospital.

Daughter
No, Dad, people use wheelchairs
at the airport, too.

Dad
Well, I don't need any damn wheelchair.
What do you think I am, an old man?

(Daughter acts totally stressed out. She sits down in
wheelchair.)

Daughter
Well, I could sure use it!

(Dad grabs handles of wheelchair.)

Dad
Which way to the jumbo jet?

(Daughter weakly points offstage.)

Daughter
Over there, Dad.

(Dad starts pushing Daughter offstage.)

Dad
(scat singing a popular song about flying)
Bum, bum, bum, la, la, la,
la, la, bum, bum, bum...

* * *

When I showed it to Dad, he laughed. I loved it when I made him happy.

"It's really good," he said.

However, now he wanted to do some editing–add some spice.

I had written one of the lines just to read, "I don't let anybody put their hands there except my doctor." Although I wasn't crazy about doing so, I finally agreed to add, "or maybe his cute, young nurse." That seemed to satisfy him.

As he was getting weaker and more delicate, I was trying to do anything to please him. I just wanted to keep him strong–alive.

Barbara and the class members got a big kick out of the new scene. She gave us the go-ahead to perform it at the next showcase and we started rehearsing. As usual, I was also going to do a serious scene with another class member. That had become my modus operandi.

* * *

One day, my girlfriend, Alice, made a casual remark that really surprised me.

"Lee Gale, you're an actress."

"No, I'm not," I protested, wanting her to say more.

"Yes, you are."

I continued to deny it, but she was insistent. I felt uncomfortable. It was the first time I had been identified with that word. I kept thinking about it.

That's ridiculous, I told myself, but I still kept thinking about it.

Shortly after that, Irwin, the man who had played the moose in our first showcase, approached me. He was going to be teaching a new senior, acting-for-commercials class at another location and he encouraged me to enroll. I thought about it for a few weeks and also kept thinking about what Alice had said.

I decided to sign up for Irwin's class. It proved to be a real revelation. Irwin was teaching not only how to perform in a commercial, but also the business side of acting. Several other class members had actually appeared in commercials. They had things like agents, headshots, resumes, and really seemed to know the ropes.

I began networking with them and taking notes. I went to the library and checked out books on acting, resume writing and anything else of relevance. I was fascinated by the whole thing. I was gradually learning how to promote myself in the field of acting.

One of my classmates showed me her headshots and referred me to the photographer who had taken them. She assured me he was reasonably priced, so I called him. I made an appointment and learned that he worked out of his apartment–no wonder his prices were so reasonable.

On the day of the photo shoot, my hair looked a mess no matter what I did, and I couldn't get my makeup on right. I was wrought up and really felt foolish. Who did I think I was, an actress or something?

I drove to the photographer's apartment/ studio and walked down a dank, dreary hallway. He showed me into an equally dreary living room. I would have left, except that my classmate had assured me he was legitimate and a nice guy. She turned out to be right. He was very pleasant and easy to work with.

The session was actually a lot of fun. The photographer talked to me the whole time, giving me directions and making jokes to help me relax. In about an hour, it was finished and I left–he would call me when the proofs were ready. I was starting to feel a little bit like an actress. It was strange.

About a week later, I picked up the proof sheet. There were about thirty-six tiny headshots of me, all on a single page. Each was slightly different and I hated every one. I guess you get what you pay for. They all seemed mediocre. Maybe it was me who was mediocre. What in the world was I doing? I called Dad.

"Dad, I need your help. I have my proof sheet and every picture is horrible."

"Come on over and we'll go over them."

That was Dad, always supportive. He had so many sides to him. The best part was that he was there for me when I needed him.

I arrived at Dad's apartment, proof sheet in hand. He listened patiently to my diatribe and then got out his magnifying glass. Together, we poured over the tiny photos. After a while, we narrowed them down and I picked out a few. Maybe they weren't as bad as I'd thought at first. Some might actually be passable. I really am my own worst critic.

I spent days agonizing over which ones were best, asking my friends, other family members, fellow actors and teachers for their opinions. They were all annoyed with me after a while.

I finally settled on one. The photographer gave me a copy of it and I took it to a print shop to have more copies made–cheaper that way. The technician made some minor changes to the photo on his computer such as removing stray hairs and such, but I was careful not to let him alter my appearance. I had learned in class that casting directors hate it when you come to an audition and don't look like the headshot you submitted to get the audition in the first place.

I cobbled together a resume based upon those of classmates as well as templates I'd found in acting books. It was composed entirely of the scenes I had performed in my class showcases; I had never done any other acting. There seemed to be a lot of white spaces on the page. I tried to spread my entries around as much as possible to cut down on how sparse everything looked–pretty pathetic.

There were so many decisions to make. Every little step was a learning experience.

* * *

Dad and I had been rehearsing our scene for several weeks. I'd been gathering props, as usual. I found Mother's old wheelchair and a couple of shoulder-strap travel bags in my garage. Barry dug deep into his stash again and pulled out a WWI Flying Ace type of aviator cap. It was the style also worn by barnstorming stunt pilots as well as Snoopy in the Peanuts cartoon strip.

Dad contributed his cheap, bomber-style, polyvinyl jacket that he had bought at some junk store. He loved that jacket and wore it everywhere. I couldn't convince him how dangerous it probably was, especially if he got too close to a flame. Oh, that man.

I noticed that Dad was finding it harder to take care of his daily needs. One day he called me.

"I want to move from this apartment. I don't need two bedrooms and everything is falling apart. Let's go look at some apartments."

It was true. The apartment was falling into disrepair and the management was lax in repairing things. However, I had been growing concerned for a while about Dad's ability to care for himself. Cooking, shopping and keeping the apartment tidy seemed to be harder and harder for him, even with a weekly cleaning woman. I was also afraid he might fall while bathing or burn himself when he turned on the stove. Now was the perfect opportunity.

"Dad, what about looking at some assisted living, retirement homes?"

I knew it wouldn't be received easily.

"No, I'm not ready for that," he snapped, obviously irritated at my inference.

I tried to explain myself.

"It's just a place where they make the meals and clean your room. Many are quite nice. You can still have complete independence and come and go as you please. They have lots of neat activities."

I had done my research.

"I'll think about it," he muttered, shutting off further conversation.

As I knew, things worked better with Dad when the idea came from him. I hung back, not bringing it up again. He didn't mention looking for an apartment again, either. A few weeks later, Dad called me with a bright idea.

"Maybe I should move to a retirement home. After all, if I'm going to go to all the trouble of moving, I might as well move there."

Yes, it was indeed astounding the inspired ideas Dad got sometimes.

Over the next several weeks, we visited different retirement homes. Finally, we found one that Dad liked which was conveniently located.

The move there was far less upsetting than I thought it would be. Once Dad made up his mind, he just forged ahead without looking back.

When he was settled into his new digs, Dad made friends and became the big man on campus. On acting class day, he would wait outside near the curb for me to pick him up, just like before.

It was getting close to show time again. Now, we were accomplished at it.

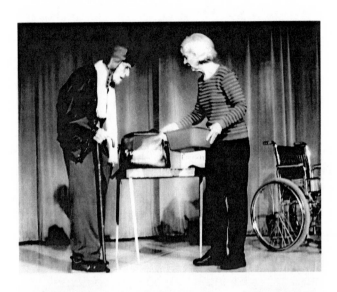

**With Dad Onstage Performing
"Going to the Airport with Dad"**

On the day of the performance, things went along without any mishaps. The last words of the scene had Dad singing the opening lines to a well-known song about flying. At rehearsals in class and at the theater, Dad would always sing it in his own fashion with the words edited as he chose. Although corrected continuously by me and other class members, he would never vary his own rendition which, I'm sure, was deliberate. I finally rewrote the ending so that he just scatted it. The truth was that he was so funny in that Flying Ace cap, he could have done anything and it would have been okay.

Again, Dad stole the show. Again, we were both high on it all. Again, we performed a few months later at Chuck's family picnic. Again, we were joyously received and barraged with congratulations.

With Dad at His Retirement Home

A few months later, a woman from an organization I belonged to asked if she could photograph Dad and me for a publication highlighting the activities of the group's members. I asked Dad, and he was delighted.

She came over to Dad's retirement home one day and Dad put on his bomber jacket and the Flying Ace cap. She took pictures of us in front of the building with some large plants as a backdrop.

I started wondering how long our adventure could continue.

CHAPTER 8
Our Fourth Scene:
"Dad Goes Mod"

In possession of second-class headshots and a pathetic resume, I began submitting them to agents from the list I had compiled from class members. I also learned about an acting newspaper, *Backstage West*, from my class. It had casting notices posted for auditions, and I found one that might be right for me. It was an open call—just show up and try out—so I decided to go to it. The audition was for the part of an aging spinster in Agatha Christie's play, *Ten Little Indians*. It was going to be held at a theater in Glendale, about twenty-five miles from where I lived..

I had read that it's often advisable to attend an audition dressed as the character you're going to portray. I tore around the house opening every closet I had in order to search for stereotypical, aging English spinster clothes. I came up with a mid-calf tweed, A-line skirt; a long-sleeve silk shirt that buttoned up to the neck; and flat, sensible, laced shoes. I dug out an old pair of horn-rimmed glasses and tied a scarf in a bow around my neck. As the final touch, I flattened my curly hair as much as possible, pinning it down with bobby pins. I was ready.

It took me about an hour to get to the theater–another maiden voyage in my acting odyssey. Again, I was extremely nervous. I walked in, took a look around, and felt ludicrous.

There were about thirty actors all over the place, waiting to audition for a variety of roles. Every one of them seemed to be dressed in jeans and a tee shirt, including the ones my age who were obviously there for the same role. I was the only one in costume. Where is that hole to crawl into when you need it?

I didn't know what I was supposed to do. I timidly asked someone and she pointed down a hallway and told me to sign in. I made my way down the narrow hallway lined with actors sitting on the floor on both sides studying scripts, gingerly stepping over the obstacle course of legs, backpacks, coffee cups, etc.

I found the sign-in sheet and entered my name. Not knowing what came next, I questioned the person closest to me.

"Just grab some sides. They're over there," he said, gesturing before returning to his script.

Where is that damned hole?

"What are sides?" I asked, while choking on the words.

Without even looking up from his reading, he simply replied, "They're a small part of the script for you to read for the audition."

He didn't laugh or look at me askance or anything else he might have done to make me feel smaller than I already felt. I guess he'd been there once, too.

I thought seriously about leaving, but another, stronger part of me wouldn't let me go. I made my way back down the hall looking for my sides where the guy had indicated. After finding them, I located a vacant piece of floor, sat down with everyone else and just began practicing my few lines.

After what seemed like hours but was probably only about thirty minutes, I was called into a room. I had no idea what to expect and my internal butterflies were working overtime. I observed about five people sitting at a long table. They just stared at me as I stood there. Again, it was book report time and I felt naked.

"She'll be your reader," a guy at the table said, pointing to a young woman standing nearby whom I hadn't seen. "Just start whenever you're ready."

I was too intimidated to ask what a reader was, so I just started to say my lines. At the appropriate point, the woman chimed in and read the lines of the other character in a bored monotone.

So, that's what a reader is—geez.

I got through the audition alive and without my throat completely freezing up. When I was finished, Table Guy simply said, "Thank you."

I walked out and practically ran to my car. Although I felt sick and stupid, that other part of me that I never quite knew existed kept saying, *At least you did it.*

That's right, at least I did it! I didn't run away; I stuck it out.

I was finally witnessing the budding fruits of all my years of struggle—my fight for self-esteem and independence. After I had become a mother, one of the various reasons I returned to work was that it was the only place where I wasn't defined by someone else. I wasn't my husband's wife; I wasn't my children's mother; I wasn't my parents' daughter. I was my own person. Working at a job saved me and strengthened me.

I called Dad right away. He wanted to know all about the audition. I told him everything, down to the ridiculous costume I was wearing. He gave me a pep talk and said he was proud of me. Dad's approval and encouragement were always the magic balm for my aching psyche. I felt much better.

I continued submitting myself for roles and started going to auditions regularly. I was gaining more confidence and knowledge about the process.

* * *

It was time to create another scene for Dad and myself. I hadn't come up with anything and Dad was getting antsy. After all, Barbara's acting class was his most important activity. I had been trying to think of a new angle for a scene, but nothing seemed to take shape.

An incident that had happened to me several months earlier had been on my mind for a long time, but I just couldn't quite seem to grasp it. I guess it must have worked its way into my subconscious.

I had been traveling on a plane–I forget where I was even going–and I happened to notice a man sitting across the aisle from me. He appeared to be Hispanic and had on a short-sleeve shirt. I noticed that he had an elaborate tattoo on his arm. I was casually admiring the workmanship of the tattoo when I saw that it had a few words in Spanish around the outside of it.

I speak Spanish and was trying to translate them to myself. They said: "El Ceurpo, La Alma, El Espíritu."

I kept staring at his arm–something looked strange. I thought the words translated as: The Body, The Soul, The Spirit. However, the Spanish word for body is "cuerpo." I couldn't figure out what was wrong. Then, I realized that the word "Ceurpo," as it was written on the tattoo, was misspelled. A tattoo misspelled, can you imagine? How do you change that? It's forever, more or less.

Another idea I'd been toying with was what Dad had mentioned to me many times—all the preening and infighting that went on at the senior citizens center where he played Bridge. Each senior strutted his/her stuff in front of members of the opposite sex. It sounded more like high school instead of a bunch of mature adults. I guess it never ends, no matter how old you get.

On a different note, Dad called me one day, talking non-stop.

"Can you believe it? I was propositioned by this young gal."

It had happened while he was taking his usual walk. She had approached him and said something about being available to show him a good time.

That's just what I wanted to hear about from my father. Is there a stronger word than "embarrassed" to describe when your father starts discussing his sexuality?

Dad couldn't stop telling that story. Of course, he didn't realize that she was probably a prostitute and just wanted his money. He told the story to anyone who would listen, and it was hard not to listen to Dad when he cornered you. I would cringe when he'd launch into it yet again. I'd try to change the subject each time he'd bring it up, but Dad was having none of my feeble efforts. He was going to be a sexy guy whether I liked it or not.

I guess it was just an offshoot of Dad's long-time love of telling dirty jokes. He thought he was so clever and sophisticated. Let me assure you, listening to one's father tell a dirty joke is the pits. For self-preservation, I'd tune out when he'd start to tell one for the umpteenth time. I'd try to change the subject, diverting his attention to something else, but why did I even waste my energy? When Dad was on a roll, no matter what it was, there was no stopping him.

My subconscious started working like a cement mixer, grinding together the senior citizens center material with my tattoo incident and Dad's "proposition" story. The idea of a theme for our next scene involving Dad being a stud and attracting all the senior ladies began to emerge. I sat down at my computer and wrote out in one sitting, *Dad Goes Mod*, altering the theme of the title for variety.

Here is the script:

DAD GOES MOD
By: Lee Gale Gruen

(Daughter is sitting in her living room on a couch reading a magazine. Dad enters wearing a jacket and walking with a cane. He is carrying a bag which he sets on a table. Dad has one side of his body and head turned away from Daughter.)

Dad
Hey, notice anything different about me?

Daughter
(glancing up at Dad)
No, I don't think so.

(Daughter returns to reading magazine.)

Dad
Look again.

Daughter
(looking harder)
I can't see anything different, Dad.

(She returns to reading.)

Dad
Come on, really concentrate.

Daughter
(irritated…puts down magazine and looks at Dad)
No Dad, what is it?

(Dad suddenly turns his hidden side toward
Daughter.)

Dad
Tah-dah!

(Daughter jumps up from couch, shocked.)

Daughter
Dad, you're wearing an earring!

Dad
Yah, I got my ear pierced. All the
guys are doing it. Wait until the babes
at the senior center get a load of me.

Daughter
(flabbergasted)
But Dad, don't you think
it's a little inappropriate?

Dad
Of course not!
(pause)
Why?

Daughter
(delicately)
Well, Dad, you're not quite the
stud you used to be fifty years ago.

Dad

Humph! A little Viagra in my
Wheaties and I'll be just fine,
thank you very much!

(Daughter looks shocked….pause…notices the bag.)

Daughter

Dad, what's in the bag?

Dad

Oh, I bought a new bathing suit.
Take a look.

(Daughter approaches the bag with her back to the audience. She opens the bag and removes a bathing suit without audience being able to see it. Then, she whirls around holding up bathing suit with two hands. Her mouth is hanging open.)

Dad

It's the newest rage. It's called a
thong. All the guys are wearing them.
Wait 'til the chicks see me in this.

Daughter
(shaking head and looking aghast)
I can hardly wait.

Dad
I've been going to exercise class
every morning at my retirement home.
By the time summer gets here,
I'll really be buff.

Daughter
(sarcastic)
Doing chair exercises?

(Dad glances daggers at Daughter.)

Dad
(haughty)
I've also been taking dancing lessons.
Watch this!

(Dad starts humming a tune and shaking his hind end as he turns around in a circle, sometimes with one hand in the air.)

Dad
(stops and faces Daughter)
How do you like them apples?

Daughter
(hands on hips…rolling eyes…shaking head)
Oh, brother!

Dad

Boy, I'm getting warm.

Help me off with my jacket.

(Daughter approaches Dad and helps him take off his jacket.)

Daughter

(can't believe her eyes)

Dad, you got a tattoo!

Dad

Yah. It's a Harley Davidson motorcycle tattoo. All the guys are getting them.

How do you like it?

(Daughter begins staring closely at tattoo.)

Daughter

(incredulous)

It's spelled wrong.

Dad

(horrified)

What do you mean?

Daughter

Harley! It's supposed to be spelled H-A-R-L-E-Y, not H-A-R-L-I-E.

(Dad clasps other hand over tattoo)

Dad
Oh my God! I'm ruined, I'm ruined!
The gals won't want to have
anything to do with me now.

Daughter
Calm down, Dad.

(Dad, very upset, starts walking off stage and shaking head while he continues talking. Daughter follows Dad.)

Dad
Go out and buy me a dozen,
long-sleeve shirts. Oh, my God, I'm
finished. I'll never be able to score
again. This is the end. I'll be the
laughing stock of the whole place.
My life is over. I'll have to leave town.
I'll have to become a hermit…etc, etc, etc.

(Dad continues walking toward stage wings while still lamenting. Daughter is still following him.)

Daughter
(placatingly…talking over Dad)
It's not that obvious, Dad. Probably

nobody will even notice. A lot of
people misspell tattoos. Daaaaad!

* * *

When I finally got it finished and polished, I showed it to Dad. He laughed and laughed. He loved it. We read it in class and everyone there also laughed. Barbara gave us the go-ahead for the showcase.

Dad and I immediately started rehearsing. However, he was no longer content just to read the lines with a few little edits. Now, he wanted creative input.

During the previous semester when Dad had wanted me to add some racier lines for his character in the scene we were doing, we had finally agreed to let Barbara decide. The next time we rehearsed that scene in class, Dad delivered his own newly edited version. I will always be grateful to Barbara for gently discouraging his sexy edits by maintaining that we shouldn't make any extreme changes since we were so close to the showcase performance. We could revisit Dad's idea in a different scene next time.

Dad never mentioned it again that semester. But, I knew my father and that he wouldn't forget it. Now, he was bringing it out for a second try.

Dad was convinced that he was a pretty sexy guy and that should be reflected in our scenes. I tried to ignore him, but as our rehearsals continued he kept suggesting more and more risqué lines for himself to be added to the scene. We soon had our first artistic disagreement. We argued about it and I kept trying to talk him out of it, but a sex symbol he was going to be.

I must describe what my father looked like physically by that time. He was now eighty-seven years old, about 5'4", 120 pounds, had thinning white hair, was even more stooped and walked with a cane. Now, how do you make a sex object out of a sow's ear? Ah, if only we could all see ourselves as we really are. To resolve it all, I finally wrote in some sexier lines and he was satisfied.

* * *

Dad had been an overweight man for half of his life, at least fifty pounds at the peak. In his forties, he went on another diet for the umpteenth time. However, it actually worked that time. He lost a lot of weight and managed to keep it off for the rest of his life. While he was steadily losing the weight, and for a long time afterward, that was all he could talk about.

"Don't I look terrific? My waist is now a size (fill in the blank). Look at me in this new bathing suit."

I could understand Dad's obsession with being sexy after having been a heavy man for so many years. On the other hand, I was bored with his preening.

What Dad couldn't seem to grasp was that to the world he was just a normal looking man. His fascination with his new self wasn't nearly so fascinating to others.

When I was about fourteen, Dad befriended another employee where he worked. Kyle was a much younger, very good looking and well-built man. I met him only once, along with his wife, at some company function. Kyle was kind of quiet and Dad was the personality kid. I could see why they were attracted to each other.

Dad became a mentor to Kyle who seemed to be Dad's fantasy avatar. Once again, in Dad's typical fashion, we were all regaled with constant Kyle stories–Kyle this and Kyle that.

"Poor Kyle, he has such a hard time shopping for clothes because his shoulders are so broad and his hips are so narrow."

Dad would have loved to have had such a problem. He experienced it vicariously through Kyle. But, he wouldn't shut up about it. Mother, Julie and I were ready to choke him. Although it wasn't Kyle's fault, we all grew to hate him–shades of Viacom.

One day Dad announced, "I've decided to adopt Kyle. He'll be the son I never had."

We were aghast! I didn't even know fathers did things like that. I wondered if tall, good looking men were simply more valuable than gawky, teenage girls. I don't remember Dad ever tripping over himself that way for Mother, Julie or me. Where was all that love and attention for us? Dad was such a skinflint with his money and now he was going to adopt Kyle who would split our eventual inheritance.

Mother went ballistic! I had never seen her so mad.

"I've had it with Kyle. You're not going to adopt him. You already have two children. You try something like that, Marvin, and I'll divorce you. I'll take half of everything you have. Then you can give the rest to Kyle."

For a mild, reserved woman, she knew how to hit him where it hurt. She insisted that if he wanted to be a part of our family, he had to sever his relationship with Kyle immediately.

Dad backpedaled rapidly, but it was too late. Mother had gotten a hold of it and wouldn't let go. "She had bottomed out" as the alcoholics would say. And, it didn't end there.

"I'm calling your sisters and telling them what you want to do."

Dad was always posturing in front of his sisters. There was the time Aunt Doreen and her husband, Uncle Joe, were celebrating their fortieth wedding anniversary at a restaurant with about fifty invited guests. Julie had made a large bouquet of flowers out of dollar bills as a gift from our family. Mother kept going up to the table where they sat in a vase among the other gifts, and rearranging them.

Dad wanted her to stop, and made a loud spectacle of himself.

"Leave those alone, Rose, and sit down right now!"

He had demeaned her in front of everyone. That contrasted so starkly with how he always introduced her to new people,

"This is my wife, Mrs. Schelf," as though she should be highly revered by mere virtue of being married to him.

He couldn't see that if he treated her with disrespect in front of others, that was tantamount to giving them permission to treat her that way, too. He also couldn't see how his behavior made him seem the petty one, not her.

Mother's threats proved not to be threats, and she did call Dad's sisters. Dad was mortified. He never wanted his sisters, nor any outsiders for that matter, to see any chinks in his armor. With Kyle as the impetus, Mother had not only chiseled chinks, she had carved out entire canyons.

That was the beginning of the turning of the tables in the Mother/Dad hierarchy in our household. Dad had finally pushed Mother too far, and now that the genie was out of the bottle, it wasn't going back in again.

As an insecure teenager viewing it all, it was frightening and exhilarating all at once. If Mother could discover her voice and stand up for herself, maybe I could, too.

Dad did end his friendship with Kyle and we never heard his name again.

* * *

We were into rehearsals at acting class and now I was faced with my prop problem yet again. First, I needed a Harley Davidson tattoo. Where was I going to get that? I got an idea, I'd go to a Harley Davidson store. Whoever thought that up is a merchandising genius. They have their own stores exclusively selling their merchandise. I had passed one once, so I went to find it.

I walked into another world. The store was full of customers. Never mind motorcycles, they were also selling all the appropriate riding gear as well as just about anything else you could slap a Harley Davidson logo onto. Apparently it's really tacky to ride a Harley dressed in anything other than leather with their giant winged insignia on it.

The only time I had ever seen anything close to it was years earlier when I was on vacation and visited Graceland, Elvis Presley's former home. Their gift shop had every conceivable item of merchandise for sale, all bearing Elvis' face–young Elvis, middle-aged Elvis, old Elvis. Who buys this stuff?

No one in the Harley store discovered I was a non-believer and threw me out, so I wandered around. In a little while, I came upon some Harley Davidson logo stickers. Perfect! I bought a few and cautiously made my getaway. Slinking off, I didn't want anyone to see that I'd arrived in a car and not on a Harley Davidson "hog."

Once I was home, I experimented with double-faced tape on the back of the sticker. Yes, it would adhere to skin. Dad's Harley tattoo was a reality.

Now, I just needed a g-string bathing suit for a man. Never in my life did I think I'd be shopping for such an item. But, hey, that's show biz.

I went to a local department store, but I couldn't find one in the bathing suit section. So, I went to the men's underwear department and started looking through the jock straps. Wanting to put a paper bag over my head pretty much describes that experience. It ranks right up there with my first time as a teenager buying Kotex. I sort of turned my head at an odd angle so the male salesclerk couldn't see me, I hoped.

They carried designer jock straps in red and blue that looked somewhat like bathing suits. But, each cost $39.99–way too expensive just for a prop to be used only once. Even I have my limits.

A few days later, I happened to be at Venice Beach with some friends and noticed that there were a lot of bathing suit shops there. I started looking through them and discovered one that had a bin with mismatched, women's bikini tops and bottoms, each for $5. I rejected all the flowery prints and found a thong in a royal blue. There was a slight problem, however. The crotch part was flat for a woman rather than pouchy for a man.

I brainstormed the matter silently. I certainly wasn't going to take anyone else into my confidence. I figured that I could alter it on my sewing machine—never mind that my sewing prowess was pretty much limited to straight lines on hems and the like. When my inner creative self surfaces, there's no stopping me. Actually, I'm pretty good with handicraft projects. I made the marshmallows on stick, didn't I?

When Richard was a child, I usually constructed his Halloween costumes myself. It tapped into my fascination with working with my hands. I created a Rubik's Cube—remember that?—out of a cardboard box with holes cut for the head and arms and squares of different colored paper glued to the sides. A skeleton costume made of paper bones taped to a black shirt and pants was easy. A…well, you get the idea.

One year, I asked Richard what he wanted to be for Halloween. Without a second thought, he replied, "Darth Vader." I didn't even know who or what that was.

"He's the guy in *Star Wars*, Mom. Everybody knows that."

I'd been duly chastised, and by an eight year old. What kind of a jerk was I?

The only thing to do was to take Richard to see the movie–his third time, my first–so I could see this character and figure out how to make the costume. The next week, we went with a few of Richard's friends at a hefty entrance fee. I sat there in the back of the theater with my grown-up friend, while Richard and company sat in the front row.

After working on the problem through half of the movie, I figured out how I would tackle the project. I crept down the aisle to where Richard was sitting and crouched down in front of him.

"Richard, I figured out how to make the Darth Vader costume," I whispered.

"Oh, I don't want to be Darth Vader anymore. I want to be Han Solo."

"What? Who the hell is Han Solo?"

I hadn't even been paying attention to the movie since I was so preoccupied with creating the costume. I came very close to screaming out loud in that crowded theater full of *Star Wars* fans. It's a good thing I didn't; I might have been lynched! As it was, I was getting a lot of dirty looks.

I crept back to my seat to watch and learn who this Han Solo character was. I was relieved when I figured out that the new costume would be much easier to make than a Darth Vader costume–just black pants, a black vest and a ray gun made from a paper towel core for the barrel taped at a right angle to a toilet paper core for the handle.

* * *

If I can make a Rubik's Cube and a Han Solo costume, I figured I could handle the crotch on a thong.

I bought the woman's bikini bottom and the next day attacked the pouch dilemma. Nothing quite worked. Then, I remembered that an old friend had once started out to make her daughter a wedding dress, but needed a form around which to mold the puffy sleeves. She found an oddly shaped, plastic bottle which worked just right. I began my search for the perfect plastic bottle.

After rummaging through every cupboard in my house and garage, I finally found a bottle with a particular curve that just might do it. I cut the plastic to size and smoothed the crotch section of the bikini bottom around it. That must be akin to a man making a bra.

I started pinning darts into the material, having to readjust it every time the plastic form uncontrollably popped out. That price of $39.99 was starting to look pretty cheap by then.

No, don't think like that. I'm going to see this thing through to the end.

After what seemed like hours of trial and error—somehow my projects always turn out to be much more complicated than I had imagined—I created somewhat of a puffy effect. I chose to view it as a size small. Surely, someone takes a size small, doesn't he? Although it wasn't perfect, I decided the audience would get the general idea. Anyway, I'd about had it with the whole, absurd undertaking.

While Dad and I continued to rehearse our scene, I was going out on more and more auditions and pursuing what I called my "glorified hobby." I didn't realize it, but acting was slowly morphing into a new part-time career.

**With Dad Performing "Dad Goes Mod"
at My Aunt and Uncle's Anniversary Party**

Our class showcase arrived again. We performed as always, still to cheers from the audience.

We subsequently put on our scene at my Aunt Sandra and Uncle Dan's sixtieth anniversary party. There were about a hundred invited guests and it was held in a private room at a big restaurant.

The entertainment consisted of a hired professional comedian, Uncle Dan who did a comedy routine he had created for a senior citizens group, and Dad and me. Everyone seemed to enjoy our performance and Dad was beaming. Of course, there was nothing greater than his family's approval. We had arrived!

CHAPTER 9
Our Fifth Scene:
"Dad goes Digital"

I was submitting myself for auditions several times a week and had to be available with very little notice to casting directors who were interested in seeing me for a role. Acting is a business, and the actor has to be at his "office" at all times. In today's world, a cell phone has become essential for any actor. I also started carrying my calendar book in my purse so I could make appointments immediately. Those two items constituted my portable office, enabling me to do business without delay should an opportunity arise.

As an additional bonus, I could talk to Richard, toll free. We began calling each other only on our cell phones. We both used the same cell phone company so we wouldn't be charged for the minutes we spoke. We could talk as long as we wanted without having to pay excessive charges.

Dad was the kind of person who rarely made toll calls–too expensive. When he did, he never enjoyed the conversation because he was too busy trying to wrap it up quickly so it wouldn't cost too much. His mind was always on the clock.

After the cell phone became a big part of my life, I got the inspiration that Dad should have one, too. That way he could call his grandsons toll free as well as having it in case of an emergency. I discussed it with him and he said he'd be willing to try it. I enrolled him with me in a family plan. He was ready to start his cell phone lessons.

There were problems from the beginning–did I honestly think it would be any different? The numbers and letters were too small for him to see and his fingers could barely push the tiny buttons.

He was still living in his apartment when I started all that nonsense, and it was located in an area that got poor cell phone reception. Things weren't going well.

"Hello, hello. God damn it! What's the matter with this thing?"

Slam! Another answering machine message from Dad on his new cell phone.

That was starting to become the norm. I was telling Richard about it during one of our regular phone conversations and he burst out laughing.

"David and I have been getting the same kind of messages from Grandpa, too."

Later, I found out that Julie was also a recipient of Dad's special answering machine missives.

I'd work with Dad, practicing and practicing. However, when he was alone, he just couldn't get the phone to function right.

Some weeks later, I received a strange telephone call. It was the manager of a cell phone store in Dad's neighborhood. Dad was there and the manager just wanted to verify our family plan. I couldn't imagine why Dad had gone to that store and I apologized profusely.

"Oh, please don't be concerned. Your father comes in all the time to get help with his cell phone."

Of course, I hadn't known about any of that. It was really quite humorous when you got beyond the frustration of it all. Anyway, we needed a new scene and that whole idea was just so funny.

I let it stew for a few days. Exaggerating it and turning the tables was the key. Daughter would start out as the technology expert with Dad as the neophyte, and then it would slowly reverse as the scene played out. Dad would end up the expert with Daughter confused and wondering who this man was who resembled her father a lot, but certainly couldn't be.

As before, I sat down at my computer and began to bang out a script. Again, ideas just jumped onto the screen. As the Dad character slowly became a technology expert, I had to include more and more complex terminology. I wasn't knowledgeable enough about it, so I found an advertisement in the newspaper from a local computer store. I perused it to see what they were selling and added appropriate items to the scene. I felt like a real writer, doing research for my manuscript.

Although I originally wrote it as a single scene, here is *Dad goes Digital* in its final form:

DAD GOES DIGITAL
By: Lee Gale Gruen

SCENE I
(CURTAIN OPENS)

(Dad is sitting on a couch, reading a magazine. Nearby is a desk with a plug-in telephone on it. Daughter enters carrying a bag which she hands to Dad.)

Daughter
Hi, Dad. Look what I bought you.

(Dad takes the bag, looks inside and removes a cell phone.)

Dad
What is it?

Daughter
It's a cell phone. It's
the newest thing.

(Dad points to the telephone on the desk.)

Dad
I already have a telephone
over there. I don't need it.

(Dad hands the cell phone back to Daughter as she
sits down next to him. She doesn't take it and pushes
his hand back.)

Daughter
This is different, Dad. It doesn't
have to be plugged in and you
can carry it with you wherever you go.

Dad
I don't like these new-fangled,
electronic things.
(pause)
How does it work?

Daughter
It's easy, Dad. You just push this
button to turn it on. Then you
push these buttons to dial the

number and you can see
it on this screen.

(Dad looks at the cell phone, holding it closer and closer to his face. He lifts his glasses onto his forehead and holds the cell phone at arm's length, straining to see it. He puts his glasses back down onto the bridge of his nose and again holds the cell phone closer to his face, straining to see it.)

Dad
I can't even see the numbers.
Here, take it back!

(Dad hands cell phone back to Daughter, who doesn't take it.)

Daughter
Be patient, Dad. Give it a chance.
Look, I'll call you on the cell
from your regular phone and
we can practice talking.

(Daughter approaches telephone on desk, picks up receiver and dials. It rings on cell phone that Dad is holding. Dad holds cell phone to his mouth.)

Dad
(loudly)
Hello...hello...hello!

Daughter
Hello, Dad. Hello...hello.

(Daughter notices Dad's confusion and approaches him.)

Daughter
Dad, you just hold it to your
ear, not to your mouth.

Dad
(irritated)
But how the hell can you
hear me when I talk?

Daughter
(patient)
It's strong enough to hear
your voice, even though your
mouth is not right at the phone.

(Dad looks perplexed.)

Daughter
Okay, now you try dialing me.

(Daughter returns to desk telephone.)

(Dad looks at the cell phone, holding it closer and closer to his face. Again, he lifts his glasses onto his forehead and holds the cell phone at arm's length, straining to see it. He puts his glasses back down on his nose and holds the cell phone closer to his face, straining to see it. Dad dials the cell phone in an exaggerated manner, index finger grossly tapping buttons. Telephone rings on desk. Daughter answers it.)

> Daughter
> Hello, Dad.

(Dad again holds cell phone to his mouth.)

> Dad
> (shouting into cell phone)
> Hello...hello. God Damn it,
> what's the matter with this thing?
> Here, it doesn't work right.

(Dad hands cell phone back to Daughter who doesn't take it.)

> Daughter
> (frustrated)
> I'll leave it with you, Dad.

Just practice using it.
You'll get the hang of it.

(ACTION FREEZES AS CURTAIN CLOSES)

SCENE II

(Daughter enters from back of theater and starts walking down the aisle as though she is a patron looking for a seat. Suddenly, a telephone rings. Daughter removes a cell phone from her pocket, pushes a button and puts it to her ear. She keeps walking down the aisle while talking on the phone in a strong but hushed voice, apologizing to other patrons as she passes them. She stops just in front of the stage.)

Daughter
Hello

Offstage Voice
Hello, I'm calling from the
Verizon Store in Santa Monica.
Is this Carol Marsh?

Daughter
Yes, but I'm in a theater.
I can't talk to you now.

Offstage Voice
Your father is here and I'm just
calling to confirm that you're
switching to the "Friends
and Family Calling Plan."

Daughter
(flabbergasted)
My father...what's my father
doing there? I hope
he's not bothering you.

Offstage Voice
Oh no. He comes in all the time;
he's a regular. We've been
teaching him how to use his
cell phone. Well, thank you
for choosing Verizon.

(Daughter stares at telephone receiver, perplexed and
not believing what she's just heard.)

SCENE III
(CURTAIN OPENS)

(Daughter is sitting on a chair reading a magazine.
Dad enters carrying a bag, which he puts down on the
end table next to Daughter.)

Dad
Well, I bought some new things
at Best Buy. Look at this!

(Dad pulls out one item and shows it to Daughter.)

Dad
It's a PDA.

Daughter
What's a PDA?

Dad
A Personal Digital Assistant,
of course. I can keep all of
my appointments and telephone numbers
in it and make notes to myself.

Daughter
(looking perplexed)
Oh!

(Dad pulls out another item and shows it to Daughter.)

Dad
And here's my new GPS.

Daughter
What's a GPS?

(Dad looks at Daughter in irritated manner, as though any idiot knows that.)

Dad
A Global Positioning System.
I can figure out directions and
locate any place in the world.
Don't you know anything
about anything?

Daughter
(looking more perplexed)
Oh!

(Dad pulls out a laptop computer.)

Dad
And here's the best one of all...
my new laptop computer. I'm
going to log on to one of
those computer dating services.

(Daughter just stares at Dad in amazement as he keeps talking.)

Dad

Listen, I made a list of things
I want you to buy for my computer.

(Dad pulls out a note pad from the bag. He starts walking off across stage, crossing in front of Daughter who slowly turns her head as she follows his progress. Dad is reading his list as he walks.)

(The curtain slowly begins to close as Dad keeps walking and reading from his list.)

Dad

I'll need a modem, a firewall,
an anti-virus program, more memory,
an extra-large monitor, a zip drive,
a Power Point program, a backup
hard drive, a digital camera port...

SCENE IV

(Takes place at the end of the entire show. The curtain opens to reveal the whole cast except for Dad in a line ready to take a bow. Suddenly, Dad walks on from the wings, passing across the stage in front of the cast while continuing to read from his list.)

Dad

...a surge protector, a laser printer,
a wireless mouse, a 256 meg flash
drive, an AGP video card,
an access point router, a 4
port USB hub, a graphics tablet,
a 1500 VA backup UPS,
a one gig dual channel DDR
memory, a USB adapter...

* * *

Dad loved it and couldn't wait to read it in class. Again, the teacher and class members were very receptive. However, Barbara had the inspired idea that we should break the original, one-scene script into different scenes which would occur interspersed with the scenes of the other class members. That would be a first in the history of our class showcases. She also suggested that between Scene I and Scene II, I should exit the stage door, run around the building, come in through the audience door and walk down the aisle as though I were a patron just entering the theater.

Interspersing our acts with others would give me time to do so. As I was walking down the aisle, another class member would operate a prop phone backstage to produce a ringing sound. I would answer it on my cell phone and start talking to the manager of the Verizon store as was written in the script.

I worried that some of the class members might be jealous of our being singled out for special treatment, but it never happened. Dad could do no wrong in their eyes.

We rehearsed and rehearsed. A few weeks later, while practicing our scene in class, Barbara came up with another idea. Normally, at the end of the showcase, all of the actors come onto the stage for a group bow in front of the audience. This time, we would all come out except for Dad.

We would be spread out horizontally, shoulder to shoulder as usual. As we were about to bow, Dad would walk out from the wings and across the stage in front of us, continuing to read the long list of complex technology devices which he had been reading as the curtain closed on our final scene. That had never been done in our class showcases, either, and the idea was really funny. Everyone was for it.

I went back to the ads in the newspaper for additional technology devices to add to Dad's list. I put in things I had never heard of, and I certainly didn't know how they functioned. Dad had to practice how to even pronounce some of them. I wasn't sure either, but between the two of us and some input from techie friends, we figured it out.

Next, it was prop time. Mainly, I needed technology devices. My penchant for handicrafts came in handy this time, too. I dug out an old three-ring, notebook binder. With a little tape and patience, it became a laptop computer. I found several small gift boxes and made each one a different piece of technology equipment, also with the help of some tape. For a cell phone, Dad would use his own, the one that had started all this.

Dad, who knew nothing about computers nor most electronic equipment, was having a hard time memorizing the complex terminology terms. That was easy to solve. We had all these wonderful props which would be great for concealing written prompts.

When Dad opened his "laptop computer," I had buzz words taped on the inside cover to help him with his lines. I taped more on the "technology devices," and planned to hand them to him in such a way that he could see the words but the audience couldn't. It took a lot of choreographing, but it worked.

I structured the script so that at the end of Scene III and at the curtain call, Dad's character was carrying a list of technological devices he wanted daughter to buy for him. He would simply read from that list.

* * *

While Dad and I were attending class, I was still going to auditions. I had recently tried out for a small play, *Dining Out*. It was written, directed and produced by Anne O'Connor on a shoestring budget. A few weeks later, Anne requested that I return for a callback. Following most auditions, casting directors often call back for another script read those actors whose performances they liked. Other interested parties who hadn't been there the first time often attend, also. Those are usually the "money men" or financial backers of the production.

The *Dining Out* callback was coincidentally scheduled on the same day as my forty-fifth high school class reunion, which was going to be a picnic lunch at a local park. I would have just enough time to spend a few hours at the reunion, leave early and rush off to the callback.

I went to the reunion and it was so much fun seeing some people whom I hadn't seen in decades. However, my mind was on the callback. An old classmate who was still my friend arrived. She knew I had gotten my first callback ever, but she was a little hazy on the details.

"Did you get the part?" she shouted from about ten feet away when she saw me. A group of people standing nearby turned and focused their attention on me for the first time.

"Are you an actress?" one of them asked. How odd it sounded. I didn't know how to answer. I kind of was and I kind of wasn't. The word "yes" came out of my mouth. I was starting to wear that label—actress. It all felt so strange.

I left the class reunion early and drove to the callback—another maiden voyage in the acting world and again I was nervous. I arrived and sat down in the waiting room. A while later, Anne called me in and gave me a different script to read than the one at the first audition. But, this time she played the other role—my reader. When we finished, she offered me the part. I was speechless.

We walked out together into the waiting room which was filled with actors who had come for their callbacks.

"I've just booked our first actor," Anne announced to the entire group.

I looked around to see who she was talking about. Wait a minute, it was me. Everyone clapped. It was a real turn on.

The play was structured as a series of mostly monologues. The characters were people one encounters in restaurants: employees and customers. It was to be staged at a small black-box style theater—the actors perform on the actual floor of the room and the audience sits in tiered seats around the perimeter.

I was not going to be paid, but who cared? It was my first real acting job. A lot of actors work in small theater and film productions for free in order to gain experience, like an apprenticeship.

I called Dad from my car on my very handy cell phone, of course. He had been waiting to hear from me and was as excited as if it had happened to him. That's all he could talk about for days. Rehearsals for *Dining Out* weren't going to start until after our class showcase. I was relieved because I already had too much going on.

It was getting close to the showcase. Dad and I were ready. We were comfortable with the routine; there were very few surprises. My anxiety level was controlled because I knew what to do. We continued rehearsing and soon it was the day of the showcase. As usual, we drove to the theater and unloaded our props.

Before the performance even started, people in the audience who had seen our scenes in previous showcases, began inquiring about Dad. They were anxious to see him perform again. He had his own fan club.

Our split-scene performance went off just right. Dad was a big hit at the unique curtain call. After he walked across the entire stage reading his list and into the far wings, he returned to the stage, waved to the audience and took his place in the middle of the line where the actors had parted to make room for him. Afterward, our friends and family members encircled us as they typically did.

However, this time there were strangers in the group. Although they had been invited by other actors, they wanted to get close to Dad and talk to him. He enchanted everyone, and he relished it.

After saying our goodbyes, we left. As I was driving Dad back to the retirement home, I could tell he was really tired. His energy level was decreasing and these performances were hard on him. Of course, he wouldn't admit it. He loved it and he knew that I loved performing with him. He would never disappoint me if he could help it.

CHAPTER 10
Our Sixth Scene:
"Going to the Market with Dad"

It was summer time and my acting class with Dad was on break. However, my real play was about to start rehearsals. Anne had scheduled our first meeting. Twenty-six cast members showed up. Most of them were much younger than I and seemed to have a lot more acting experience.

Anne didn't even discuss the play. She said we were going to do an acting exercise. We sat around in a circle on the chairs we had brought at her request.

She handed out two pieces of paper to each of us with a character and one line of dialogue written on the first, and another line of dialogue on the second. We couldn't look at our papers until it was our turn. We had to portray our character through improvisation, working in the first line of dialogue. Then, when we were almost finished, we were to look at the second paper and use that line of dialogue before finishing our performance.

When it was my turn, I looked at my first paper and I was stumped. I was to portray a race horse. Others had portrayed some pretty strange things, but a race horse had to be the worst.

After a few moments of deliberation, I decided to just go for it. I began galloping around the floor, whinnying and snorting while uttering the obligatory line—not bad, I was doing okay. When I got tired of galloping, I looked at the second paper to find out what my final line would be.

"I salute you," I snorted, horse-like.

Then, without really thinking about it, I lifted one of my legs a little out to the side and made a loud, whooshing noise as though I were peeing.

Everyone started laughing. Some actually laid down on the floor and rolled around in hysterics. Being in my sixties and rather poised in my manner and appearance, it seemed so out of character that it really broke the ice. After that, all the younger actors were able to loosen up and stop behaving in such a guarded way around me.

Anne handed out our scripts after we finished the improv exercise. When I saw my monologue, I couldn't believe I'd ever be able to memorize the whole thing. It was one page, single spaced and took four minutes to deliver. That's a lot of dialogue and a long time to be talking alone onstage.

After that, we did a table read—we read through the script without any props or blocking. The script was really good and I loved my role. I was to be a wealthy, snobbish woman who, while her flat tire is being repaired, goes to a nearby "greasy spoon" restaurant well below her standards and complains the whole time.

I worked very hard on memorizing my lines. I wanted to keep up with the others and not let Anne down. We had rehearsals several times a week, always at night. I was beat but exhilarated when I got home. Once, our rehearsal ran until 2:00 am. I learned that it takes a lot of stamina to be an actor.

It was gratifying to be working with good dialogue and accomplished fellow actors. Anne was strict, but also supportive and caring. We all respected her and did our best for her.

We were finally ready to put on the production. I had invited everyone I knew. Dad came with Julie on opening night.

The actors were all in the dressing room applying makeup, changing into costumes, running lines and a million other things. It was another first in my acting life and I was reveling in it.

Putting on my stage makeup brought up a painful memory. When I was in junior high school, Mother gave me my first lipstick, a small sample size she had gotten free somewhere. I have a very fair complexion and must use mascara and eyebrow pencil to make my eyes stand out. Lipstick alone just emphasizes my mouth while the rest of my face all blends into one washed-out hue.

The first day I wore lipstick to school, one of the girls in gym class took a look at me and made her pronouncement.

"You look like a clown. Let's call her clowny."

All the other girls took up the chant and wouldn't let up. I was humiliated and kept biting my lip to stop from crying in front of them. They continued it on and off over the next few weeks. Of course, I stopped wearing lipstick and didn't use makeup again for some years, and then in a carefully controlled, pale-colored palette. Now, here I was applying my stage makeup thickly and in bright colors so I could be seen easily by the audience—so ironic.

It was time. Anne called places and we waited in the wings for our cue. When it came, we all began marching across the stage for the group opening scene, and then back to the wings to wait for our individual monologues. I kept going over and over my lines, mostly to calm myself and keep my focus.

Periodically, I would glance at the actor who was to perform just ahead of me as a reminder to get ready for my entrance. When he went onstage, I took my place in the wings and watched him the whole time. As he exited, I walked out trying to stay in character and ignore the audience. Once I started talking, it became a lot easier. I was learning to discipline my mind and not let it wander.

My monologue flew by. As I was leaving the stage, the next actor was walking on just as we had rehearsed. What a relief. Although scared, I had done it.

Dad and I joined forces after the curtain call. Our friends and family gathered around us and made a big fuss over me, and over Dad by extension, of course. It was pretty heady stuff.

In about the middle of the *Dining Out* run, Richard flew in just to see me perform. He always loved to tease me and threatened to make a spectacle when I came onstage.

"If you do, I'll jump ten feet in the air and land on your throat."

It was one of our favorite threats to each other. There is nothing worse for a stage actor during a performance than to be distracted from living in the scene. It is doubly worse when done deliberately by a well-meaning friend. Once, a few years later, while I was onstage in a play, a friend in the audience waved to me with a big smile on his face. I knew it was done innocently and he only wanted to let me know he had come to see me perform, but it threw off my concentration and I could have killed him.

Of course, Richard didn't make a spectacle and was very respectful as an audience member. I saw him anyway, sitting in the middle section, but I forced myself to go back to my focus. I would glance at him from time to time and could tell he was really enjoying watching me.

Richard was a bit of an entertainer himself, an amateur, self-taught juggler. There are a few precious moments involving his juggling that remain in my mind.

Years earlier when we were visiting Natalie at her placement, Richard picked up three small pinecones from the ground and started walking around the patio juggling them. The residents, all disabled like Natalie, were enchanted. They followed him like a marching band leader as he strolled.

Another time, Richard and I were traveling together in Europe after he had graduated college. One day we came upon two men in a park juggling objects back and forth. Richard walked over and gestured that he wanted to cut in. One guy stepped aside and Richard took his place for a while before turning it back over. No words were exchanged. Richard and the jugglers didn't even speak the same language. Some communication is just universal.

After the curtain call, Richard ran up and hugged me. It was the first time he had seen me perform as an actress and he couldn't believe it–his mother. Due to his commitments, he had to fly back that same night, but at least he had come.

The show was originally scheduled to run for eight performances, short by most standards. After a brief extension, it eventually closed. It's too bad that it couldn't have continued longer because it was so good, but that's all the budget would allow. It was sad to say goodbye to Anne and the other cast members. We had become like a family.

Anne had printed up posters to advertise the show. I framed one and hung it on my wall at home. I was starting my own rogues gallery of my new career.

My acting accomplishments were giving me more confidence in myself than I had ever had in my life. It was incredibly liberating. Many of my hang-ups were slowly dissolving. I loved it and wanted more. Eat your heart out, stage fright.

* * *

It was time to write another scene for Dad and me. My thoughts started wandering.

Occasionally, when Dad would pull one of his outlandish antics, I'd just smile and wag my finger at him.

"Go ahead. You'll just see that in the next scene I write."

He'd look at me, suddenly mute. Eureka! I had found an antidote. We'd both laugh—still more bonding.

In her later years, Mother had also found a Dad-antidote. Once, she had gotten so mad at him that she took off her prescription glasses and threw them across the room, breaking one of the lenses. Since she needed her glasses, they had to be repaired which meant that Dad had to pay for it. She had gotten him where it hurt.

After that, all Mother had to do when she got upset with Dad was to take off her glasses and start shaking them menacingly.

"Okay, Rose, calm down," he'd counsel, suddenly the cool and collected one.

It's too bad Mother hadn't thought of that years earlier. She and I would laugh about it in private as she practiced her "glasses-shaking technique."

As my mind was sorting through different themes for our next scene, I began to think about an incident that Dad and I had been involved in a few years earlier. We had gone shopping at a small neighborhood produce market that Dad loved. It was cheap–the only criterion. He insisted it had the best prices anywhere around, never mind that most of the merchandise was overripe.

We wandered around, filled our cart and paid for our purchases. I told Dad to take the shopping cart out of the back door into the parking lot while I went to get the car. I had parked about a block away as there was nowhere to park in the market parking lot–it was popular with all of Dad's crowd. The plan was to meet him at the back door, load the bags of groceries into the car and leave.

When I got there, I didn't see Dad. I couldn't imagine what had happened.

I was able to find a place in the lot to park the car temporarily. I rushed in the back door and saw him just inside, struggling with the shopping cart.

"What's the matter with this damned thing?"

Although he was pushing it with all his strength, it refused to budge. The cart finally started progressing at a snail-pace as Dad struggled mightily. Neither one of us could understand it. The cart was close to the back door and nothing seemed to be obstructing it. It was as though a giant invisible hand had reached down and held it captive. By that time Dad was completely flustered and swearing repeatedly.

"Settle down, Dad," I pleaded to no avail.

I examined the shopping cart. It had a long vertical metal pole bolted to the handle to prevent it from clearing the doorway so people couldn't remove it from the premises. But, the cart was several feet from the door and the pole wasn't even in contact with the doorframe.

I looked up and saw that the ceiling began to slope gradually downward toward the back door. When Dad had walked in that direction, the pole made contact with the sloping ceiling. As he continued to push the cart, the pole began scraping, carving an ever deepening groove. I felt like a kid who has been caught stealing. There was the evidence: a long, ugly gash in the ceiling.

"Dad, stop pushing."

Well, forget it. Dad was temperamental and had complete tunnel vision. He was going to get that blasted cart out of the door if it killed him. Mother used to say that he was so single-minded, you had to hit him over the head with a brick chicken house to get his attention.

I was waiting for the store manager to descend upon us at any moment and demand payment for the damage. After much effort, I directed Dad's attention toward the ceiling while trying not to attract anyone else's attention there—a neat trick with our theatrics going on.

Dad quickly got the picture and became very circumspect. He, too, realized there might be a monetary penalty involved, and that was anathema to him. Why were we at that crummy store anyway buying distressed fruit, only to pay big bucks for repairing its ceiling?

A box boy out in the parking lot apparently had seen Dad having a tantrum while fighting with the shopping cart. I'm sure he was aware that the carts weren't allowed out of the store. Nevertheless, probably to avoid alarming other customers, he grabbed the opposite end of our cart and picked it up, thereby forcing the handle with the pole to tilt downward. Then, he pulled the cart out of the door as the pole cleared the doorframe, closely trailed by Dad and me.

I hurriedly loaded Dad and the groceries into the car which still had the engine running. I guess I must have anticipated needing to make a fast getaway. After all, you never know what's going to happen when you're with Dad. I jumped in the driver's seat, put the car in gear, gunned the motor and sped off, leaving the cart, the box boy, the market and the ceiling gash in our dust.

"Let's get the hell out of here," Dad shouted as we peeled rubber.

We hightailed it out of there like a couple of bandits being chased by a posse. A few blocks later, the adrenaline wore off and I burst out laughing. Dad caught it and started laughing, too. I stopped the car since I was in no condition to drive. We were both totally out of control, laughing like kids who had snatched some fruit from a stand and run off.

That incident became the germ for our next scene. But, I still needed more.

Dad had told me about various markets where he shopped because they had such wonderful freebies. One had bakery samples, another had cheese samples, etc. Dad knew them all–his haunts. I decided to incorporate this, also, into *Going to the Market with Dad*.

Here is the first script I wrote:

GOING TO THE MARKET WITH DAD
By: Lee Gale Gruen

(Dad and Daughter enter a market. Dad starts to push a shopping cart. Tables are spread around the stage, each with a different sign on it saying: Dairy, Bakery, Cereal, Produce, Medication and Automated Cashier. Some tables have trays of free samples.)

Dad
Well, this is the new Gelson's Market
that I told you about. Isn't it huge?

Daughter
Yeah, this is really something.

Dad
Come on over here. They have
lots of free samples.

(Dad points to the dairy table and starts walking toward it with Daughter following behind. He takes two toothpicks from a dispenser on the table and spears a cube of cheese on each from the sample tray on the table, handing one to Daughter.)

Dad
Here, try some of this cheese.

(Dad and Daughter eat their cheese.)

Dad
Isn't it delicious? I had some when
I was here yesterday.

Daughter
Yeah!

(Dad removes a baggie from his pocket, grabs a handful of the cheese samples, puts them in the baggie and puts the baggie into his pocket.)

Daughter
(shocked)
Dad, I don't think you're supposed to
take so many. They're for everyone.

Dad
Oh, don't worry. They expect it.

(Dad starts pushing the shopping cart toward the bakery table. He gestures toward Daughter.)

Dad
Come on over here.

(Daughter follows Dad to the bakery table. Dad takes two small slices of cake from the sample tray on the table and hands one to Daughter.)

Dad

Here, try this cake. I had a piece
yesterday and it was delicious.

(Dad and Daughter eat their cake samples. Dad takes a baggie out of his pocket, grabs a handful of cake slices, puts them into the baggie and puts the baggie into his pocket.)

Daughter
(embarrassed)
Dad, don't take all those. They're meant
for the other customers, too.

Dad
Oh, don't worry. They have plenty.
Come on over here.

(Dad starts walking toward the cereal section with Daughter following. He takes a box of cereal, tears open the top and begins eating cereal from the box. He offers the box to Daughter.)

Dad
Here, try some of this.

Daughter
(flabbergasted)
Dad! You're not supposed to
tear open packages!

Dad
Oh, don't worry. Everyone does it.
Come on over here.

(Dad starts walking toward the produce table with Daughter following. He grabs a bunch of grapes and starts eating a few. Then, he offers the bunch to Daughter.)

Daughter
Dad, these aren't free samples. I
don't think we're supposed
to eat the whole bunch.

Dad
Oh, don't worry. It's not a big deal.
Ah, hand me a bag, will you? I want
to buy a pound of apples.

(Daughter hands Dad an empty bag. Dad puts about four apples into the bag and puts the bag into the shopping cart. Suddenly, he grabs his stomach and begins moaning.)

Dad
Oh, I'm getting a stomachache.
I think I ate too much. I know what to
do. Come on over here.

(Dad starts pushing the shopping cart toward the medication table with Daughter following. He picks up a bottle, opens it, pours a few pills into his hand and puts them into his mouth.)

Dad
Thank God for Tums.

Daughter
Dad, you're not supposed
to do that!

Dad
Oh, don't worry, nobody will miss
a few. Come on, let's go to the cashier
so I can buy these apples.

(Dad and Daughter walk to the automated cashier table.)

Dad
Have you seen this? It's the newest thing.
You just put your bag on the counter
and it automatically tells you how

much it costs.

(Dad puts the bag of apples on the table. Suddenly, he looks at the automated cashier, furious.)

Dad
(shouts)
What...a $1.29 for a pound of
apples? That's a hell of a nerve you
have charging prices like that.
Who do you think you are?

(Daughter grabs Dad's shoulder.)

Daughter
Calm down, Dad. You're
talking to a machine.

(Dad turns toward Daughter while pushing her hand away.)

Dad
Will you be quiet! Can't you see
I'm trying to talk to this machine?

(Dad turns back to automated cashier and pushes the bag of apples away to far end of table.)

Dad

Here, you can just keep your
Goddamn apples! I don't want them.

(Dad turns toward Daughter.)

Dad

Let's get out of here!

(Dad starts walking off stage with Daughter following. Dad is loudly mumbling to himself.)

Dad

See if I ever shop here anymore!
That's highway robbery! Wait until I
tell all my friends! We'll put them
out of business! There are a lot of
other stores I can go to!....etc, etc, etc.

* * *

Dad, Barbara and the class gave their approval for the script. We went on to rehearsals, as usual. We were familiar with the drill and easily fell into it.

By this time Dad was eighty eight and extremely frail. He was quite wobbly on his feet, even when using his new four-footed cane. Everyone in class had become very protective of him. I'm sure they, too, saw him deteriorating.

* * *

Years earlier, Richard had been accepted into a study-abroad program as part of his college undergraduate studies at the University of California at Berkeley. He was to spend his junior year at a university in New Zealand.

Dad and I took him to the airport for his departure. He was leaving a month early so he could island-hop on the way, visiting various Pacific islands before arriving at his final destination. We were worried about him. He had never done anything like that before. Would he survive?

Dad never showed his concern openly. He only encouraged Richard and told him how proud of him he was.

I looked at Dad's face and it mirrored my own.

"I'm sure he'll be okay," was all he said.

"Yeah," I responded softly.

We watched Richard as he disappeared down the hallway toward the plane. We stayed there a long time afterward, not speaking, just thinking our shared thoughts.

I felt the same way I did the first time I had let Richard walk to school by himself. I followed him to make sure he was safe. I hid behind bushes and walls so he wouldn't see me and think that I doubted his ability. Could I follow him onto the airplane to New Zealand? Maybe I could hide in the cockpit.

Now I was doing the same with Dad. I'd walk behind him, careful so he wouldn't realize I was watching him. Could I hold Dad up? Could I somehow become his crutch?

One of my classmates noticed me watching Dad one time.

"I'm sure he'll be okay," she said, trying to reassure me.

"Yeah," I responded softly.

I knew it couldn't go on forever, but whenever those thoughts crept into my mind, I'd crowd them out using my usual modus operandi–busyness. Every so often, in spite of myself, my mind would drift into thoughts of how and when this acting partnership would end.

The phone was ringing. Was I dreaming? What time was it? It seemed like the middle of the night.

"Your father has fallen and was taken to Brotman Medical Center in Culver City," said some woman.

Everything became surreal. I got dressed and drove to the hospital, all in someone else's body.

I scrambled around and found Dad in a hallway lying on a gurney. He was rational and talking calmly, comforting me instead of the other way around. That was Dad, always in charge, even while flat on his back.

He had broken his hip while undressing in his room, tripping over his pant legs as he tried to step out of them. He summoned help by pressing the button on the Life Line bracelet he had taken over from Mother after she died. He'd have to have an operation to insert a rod and pin into the broken hip. Dad already had everything figured out.

"Go to my room and get my three metal boxes out of the closet."

They were the ones where he kept all of his important papers. He had shown them to me often so I would know where they were.

I was then to arrange with the retirement home management to hold his room for him until his anticipated return, but not charge him for it. Dad was always playing the angles.

Yeah, fat chance, I thought but didn't verbalize.

Dad had numerous other instructions for me. I knew that he was scared and it was his only way of coping–to get very busy and stay in total control. I was definitely my father's daughter.

After the surgery, Dad was transferred to a rehabilitation nursing home to recover. He started daily physical therapy sessions with the assistance of a physical therapist, Shawn. Dad walked with a merciless limp, but he had that look of determination so typical of him as he soldiered on.

When I'd visit during physical therapy time, I'd walk behind them. Shawn would hold onto Dad by a thick supportive belt around Dad's waist as he struggled to walk with the aid of a walker. It pained me to watch. I'm glad he couldn't see my face, because he tried so hard, day after day.

Shawn was an aspiring actor himself–isn't everyone in Los Angeles? He really liked Dad and would hang around him whenever he wasn't busy working elsewhere. Of course, they'd talk acting–what else?

I have become aware that acting is like an addiction. If you're bitten by the bug, that's all you want to eat, breathe and talk about 24/7. When I'd visit, Shawn, Dad and I would talk the talk, connecting privately to the exclusion of everyone else.

Shortly after Dad first entered the nursing home, he insisted that we should continue practicing our scene. We had been a few months into rehearsals when he broke his hip.

"I can perform in my wheelchair."

"Well, why not?" I thought.

I could just rewrite a few things, reposition the props and we'd be okay. I did just that.

Instead of Dad walking with a shopping cart, he would be sitting in a wheelchair being pushed by Daughter. He would hold in his lap one of those plastic hand-held baskets that markets provide for their customers. This time, Dad would put the free samples into the basket instead of his pocket. The revisions were simple enough and worked just as well with the story.

I started gathering props. Mother's old wheelchair, now Dad's, was going to be used again in one of our scenes–this time out of necessity. I needed a hand-held basket for Dad's lap. I went to a neighborhood market where I often shopped, and asked to borrow one. When I explained the situation, the manager was very cooperative. He told me just to return it when I was done. Even in crass Los Angeles, some people are still so generous.

I made signs to sit atop TV trays which would represent the different sections of the market. I planned to position the trays in two rows to form an aisle between them. I could push Dad in his wheelchair down the middle from one tray to the next.

I would stock each table with the free samples that we were going to eat. As in past scenes we had performed, it took a lot of choreographing and my handicraft skills, but I was totally energized by it. Dad and I discussed it in great detail each day, and he had lots of input, of course.

Dad was not able to attend class anymore, but he and I continued rehearsing at the nursing home. During our first rehearsal there, he couldn't get out of bed because he was still very weak from the surgery and hadn't started his physical therapy yet.

I crawled into Dad's narrow hospital bed with him and we laid side-by-side, each holding up one edge of the script between us as we read our lines.

Shawn walked in while we were at it and stopped, speechless. He just stood there watching us, not breaking the spell. I think that's when he first fell in love with Dad.

I was still progressing deeper and deeper into the acting world. I had learned about online casting websites from other cast members in *Dining Out*. I sat in front of my computer for hours, figuring out how to post my headshots and resume online so that I could submit myself for even more acting roles.

I told Dad about each new experience. We'd troubleshoot it for hours. I think it really invigorated him. Later, he'd tell Shawn all about it.

On the day of the showcase, I went to the nursing home to pick up Dad. That, too, was a challenging choreography act. I had to collapse the wheelchair, disassemble the leg rests and load them all into the trunk of my SUV. Fortunately, the back seat folded down to allow plenty of room. After that, I had to help Dad maneuver himself into the passenger seat–a major feat–and buckle his seat belt.

When we arrived at the theater, I had to do everything again in reverse. Then, I had to wheel Dad into the theater and return to retrieve the props. Several of my classmates and some of my friends who had come early were more than willing to help. Nevertheless, I was pretty tired by then. I never let on because Dad was so thrilled by it all. What I was doing was actually a continuation of my ongoing gift to him, and to myself.

Dad got lots of attention from all the class members who had not seen him for a few months since he broke his hip. He was his old self again, at least for the moment. Only I knew how much it was taking out of him. He had lost a lot of strength since his surgery. But, Dad being Dad, he rose to the occasion and was joking and acknowledging everyone.

The audience thought that Dad sitting in a wheelchair was part of the scene. I pushed him down the aisle between the TV trays and he held the shopping basket on his lap. As we approached the different trays with their identifying signs, there was a plate on each with the free samples. So far, the scene was playing out just as I had re-written it.

Dad was supposed to offer me one sample and then take a few more and put them into the shopping basket on his lap. That was in the script and that is what we had rehearsed in his hospital room.

Well, what does a script have to do with anything when it comes to my father? Instead, after offering me one of the samples, he simply picked up the whole plate and dumped the rest of them into his shopping basket. I was really annoyed until I heard the audience laughing. Once again, Dad had called it right.

When the curtain call was over and all the props were in my car, I had to repeat my previous routine of loading Dad and the wheelchair back in. We drove to the nursing home, both totally spent.

**With Dad Onstage Performing
"Going to the Market with Dad"**

Once he was helped into bed by the staff, I kissed him goodbye and returned to my car. As I was driving home, I realized that today had been Dad's last performance. Another door had closed.

Dad's nephews had come to the showcase and filmed our scene. They emailed it to all the relatives including their sister who was living in Thailand. The entire family called to congratulate Dad. He was so moved, and, of course, told Shawn about it. Dad had impressed his family and proven his rejecting father wrong, once again.

CHAPTER 11
Dad in the Nursing Home

"I want to have a talk with you and your father," Shawn said over the telephone.

It sounded ominous, but I figured it was probably just more acting chatter. I arrived a few hours later and Shawn came into the room. He bent down in front of Dad, who was sitting in his wheel chair.

"The physical therapy isn't working, Marvin. You're not going to be able to walk again," Shawn was saying in what seemed like slow motion. "Now it's time to learn to use your wheelchair by yourself."

Dad and I were reeling.

Thank you, Shawn, for being so honest, I thought, *but can't you reconsider?*

How ridiculous we human beings are when we get into denial mode. Shawn wasn't God. He was just a man delivering terrible news to another man he adored.

Dad was crushed, I could tell. But he didn't let on, at least to Shawn. I knew by his silence, which was totally out of character for him. If Dad was quiet, something was wrong.

Dad rallied as the days progressed. He threw his energy into learning to propel himself forward in his wheelchair by using his heels on the floor in a walking motion.

When he couldn't negotiate a slight incline in the hallway, he practiced turning his chair around, again with his feet, and pushing them against the floor to roll up the slope backwards, just like Shawn had taught him.

Dad became very adept at his new mode of transportation and spent long periods of time cruising the hallways. When I'd visit, we would "take a walk" together. As often as not, if I stopped to chat with someone, when I'd look back, Dad was nowhere to be seen. I would have to search the adjoining hallways and recreation room to find him.

Speedy Gonzales, I thought.

It was heartwarming and heartbreaking, all at the same time. Dad was an inspiration. He rarely complained and simply made the best of what life handed him.

Over the next two years, he continued to go downhill. I, on the other hand, was going uphill. My glorified hobby was turning into another career and taking over my life–my "second act."

I enrolled in another senior, acting-for-commercials class, taught by a wonderful teacher, Buddy Powell. I worked on improving my ability to perform in front of a camera. I learned how to stress certain words and phrases in a commercial script–especially the name of the product. I also had an opportunity to practice using a teleprompter. I had new headshots taken that were much more flattering than the previous ones.

Dad insisted upon having one of the photographs as soon as they were ready. When I arrived at the nursing home a few weeks later with the coveted object in hand, Dad called in all of the nursing staff to view the unveiling. He was certainly the resident personality kid there; his natural charisma drew people to his room.

I had nailed a bulletin board to the wall opposite Dad's bed. It was positioned so he could see all of the family photographs thumb-tacked there as soon as he opened his eyes in the morning.

"Put your picture in the middle."

With careful deliberation, he directed me exactly where to tack up each of the other smaller, family photographs. He was definitely going to be his own interior decorator. The whole arrangement looked like the sun with the planets revolving around it.

As the months went by, Dad developed other serious health problems. We had originally thought the nursing home would be temporary, only until he recovered from the hip surgery. We gradually became aware that it was going to be his permanent place of abode.

"This is my home now. These are my friends," Dad proclaimed one day, referring to the nursing home staff and some of the more lucid residents.

Dad was a realist and didn't deceive himself. He soon adjusted to his situation and made the best of it. I bought him a television set with some plug-in earphones to help him hear the sound better, just like he used to have when he lived in the apartment. I would arrive and see him sitting up in bed, wearing his earphones. He looked so sweet and innocent, like a child. I'd give him a hug and kiss, and we'd laugh together.

Dad lived for the next two years in the nursing home. He was never able to come to another acting class or showcase. I, on the other hand, continued attending class and partnered with others for the showcase scenes. I'd always rehearse my lines with Dad and he would play the other part. He liked his job as my reader.

I also continued going on auditions and submitting myself for new roles. About a month after Dad had his operation, I got a call from a talent agent. She had seen my headshot and resume on one of the internet casting websites and noticed that I didn't have an agent. She offered me commercial representation.

I was so surprised, I didn't know what to say. The agent wasn't requiring me to sign a contract, so I agreed. I figured I didn't have anything to lose and maybe something to gain.

I went to visit Dad later that afternoon and we huddled together to discuss all of the possible ramifications. He felt that I had made the right decision. Within a few months, I booked my first paid acting job, a commercial which would pay me $400. Actually, it was only offered to me by default. The role called for my character to roller-skate down the sidewalk carrying the sign of the sponsoring company. I had noted on my resume that I could roller-skate, although in truth, I hadn't done it in years. I didn't have to demonstrate my skating ability at the audition, so I went. However, I didn't get the job.

A few days before the shoot, my agent called. The actress who was initially hired had fallen down and injured herself when she tried to skate. Now, they wanted me.

The director told me to purchase some skates in my size and agreed to reimburse me for the cost. I rushed off to the nearest sporting goods store to search for roller skates. I didn't even know if I could stand up in them. The salesclerk who waited on me introduced himself as Igor.

"Igor, I have to learn to skate on these things, and I haven't skated in years," I told him. "I want to practice skating around the store, and I want you to hold onto me and keep me from falling. If I can get the hang of it, I'll buy the skates from you."

I doubt that Igor had ever gotten such a request before. Nevertheless, although initially looking perplexed, he was a good sport about it and agreed. I was concerned, however, because Igor was shorter than I and looked like he weighed less. If I went flying off uncontrollably, I was pretty sure he wouldn't be able to hold me up and we'd both end up on the floor.

After launching myself, I was really unsteady. Igor was very caring, crab-stepping along while holding his arms protectively cage-like around my body.

As I progressed, I began leaning forward slightly to balance myself like I do when I'm skiing. Gradually, I got into the rhythm of it and was holding my own.

We were quite a spectacle, Igor and I. The other customers and the staff really enjoyed it all. As we circled and circled, we'd pass the same people. They tracked my improvement and shouted words of encouragement while giving thumbs-up signs. Once I felt confident enough, I gave poor Igor a hug, paid for the skates and left with my prize in hand.

The next day I had to meet the director in a parking lot to demonstrate that I could roller-skate. He wasn't taking any chances this time.

I got there early so I could practice on my own. Although I skated slowly, I was able to remain upright and move in a forward direction. There was one small catch. I couldn't master stopping. So, I developed a technique of skating toward a tree, a car, a bike rack or whatever. Upon arrival, I'd grab it and come to an abrupt halt. It wasn't pretty, but it worked.

I passed the director's scrutiny and was told where to report a few days later to shoot the commercial. I still couldn't fathom that anyone would be willing to pay me to act. Didn't they know that I'd do it for free?

Shoot day came and I arrived right on time. Everything was in motion. There were trucks, equipment, crew members, etc, all over the place. There was even an off-duty police officer to stop traffic when they filmed in the street. I had frequently seen film crews on-location around Los Angeles, but I never thought I'd be part of one. It was really something.

I changed into the clothing the wardrobe mistress gave me. Then, another crew member walked with me about a block to the street where the filming would actually take place.

The director told me I would be roller-skating first down the sidewalk and later in the street. I surveyed the site and realized there was nothing I could skate toward to stop myself. Oh brother, now what?

"Ah, I have a slight problem," I informed the director.

I explained that I was stop-challenged when it came to roller-skating.

"Don't worry about it."

He called over the makeup artist who had just recently applied my makeup, and asked her to be my "catcher." She was to stand just out of camera range and I would skate into her waiting arms–a perfect solution.

We practiced and she turned out to be just as good as trees and cars. If she can't make it as a makeup artist, she has a good future as a catcher.

When I eventually received my paycheck from my agent, I just kept staring at it. I drove over to the nursing home to show it to Dad.

"Can you believe it, Dad?"

He was speechless, and that was a rarity for my father. He just kept looking at the check and smiling and shaking his head.

I left Dad's and went directly to a photocopy store where I made a color copy of the paycheck. Then, I went to a picture frame store to buy a frame for it. They had some especially for checks and paper money. I guess I'm not the only strange one around.

After I framed the copy, I hung it in my hallway. It was Exhibit II in my acting, rogues gallery.

When I had originally composed my resume, I filled it with entries of the scenes I had done in my class showcases, since that's all I had. Slowly, as I booked parts, I replaced those first entries with real jobs. It was surprising how they were beginning to add up.

* * *

During the next few years, I had several little brushes with fame. The first time, a journalist from a small local newspaper visited Buddy Powell's acting class to write an article about it. I arrived early and sat in the front row, my usual choice. Unbeknownst to me, as the photographer was taking pictures of a class member standing upfront being interviewed along with the teacher, the entire classroom was visible behind them. When the article came out a few weeks later with a photograph accompanying it, Buddy Powell and that student were in the front, but I could be seen in a prominent location in the background.

I was also mentioned in the article quite a bit. It talked about my having been a probation officer and that I discovered acting following retirement. It went on to say that I had performed in two plays in community theater as well as in two television commercials. It quoted me talking about the camaraderie in class because everyone was so focused on their acting and not on their latest aches and pains, even though the ages of the seniors who attended ranged well into their nineties.

The following month, I was contacted by another journalist, Elizabeth Pope, who was writing an article about seniors and their second careers to be published in *Time Magazine*. She had contacted the organizer of a retired, professional women's group that I belonged to, and had been referred to me because she was looking for seniors with interesting and unusual stories. She asked if she could interview me and send a photographer to my scene study class to photograph me.

Are you kidding? Whenever you like, I thought. "That would be fine," I said calmly, carefully controlling my emotions.

Dad and I had both been subscribers to *Time Magazine* for years. This would be more fodder for his bragging rights.

Elizabeth interviewed me over the telephone. With Barbara's permission, the photographer came to the class and took pictures of me in acting-mode to accompany the article. His assistant had one of those big round reflectors that photographers use to bounce light onto their subjects, and he kept holding it near me. It was disconcerting to have someone constantly shooting pictures of me while I was trying to behave naturally and just participate in the class exercises. I never knew quite what to do.

I seemed to be the envy of everyone in the class. One of my classmates who had barely spoken to me previously, suddenly became my friend. He was all chatty, wanting to perform a scene with me. I'm sure he was hoping his picture would get into the magazine, too.

We waited anxiously for the next few months until the anointed issue came out. Dad, who received his *Time Magazine* subscription at the nursing home, called me one day.

"I've got it! Your picture is on the first page of the article. It covers about a third of the page."

My mail hadn't been delivered yet, so I hadn't seen it. The phone started ringing. Several of my friends were calling to congratulate me. I drove over to see Dad. When I arrived, he had already shown the article to everyone at the nursing home. As I walked down the hall toward his room, staff members passed by with admiring looks and congratulated me. Good old Dad; my triumph became his triumph. When I entered his room, he was talking on the telephone.

"…and her picture is in *Time Magazine*. Well, go out and buy it," he was ordering the captive party at the other end.

When Dad saw me, he grabbed the magazine which was already open to the right page and handed it to me. There I was, standing alone with a script in my hand, the photo covering about a third of the page, just like Dad had said. Wow!

My name next to the picture was messed up a little bit. They had failed to include my middle name which I always use together with my first name as though it's all one name: Lee Gale. Who cared? It was me!

The only mention of me in the general article was one line without my name, which referred to a probation officer who had become an actress. Who cared? My photograph was huge!

I continued getting phone calls from family and friends for the next few weeks. Even my cousin in Chicago saw the article and called. The class members in both Barbara's class and Buddy's class were buzzing about it, too. I rode that wave for some time.

I wanted to keep copies of the magazine. Upon my request, *Time Magazine* sent me several, uncirculated copies. Friends also gave me their copies. I cut out the article from one of them, framed it and hung it in my hallway–Exhibit III in my acting rogues gallery.

A few months later, local television personality Huell Howser came to Buddy Powell's commercial acting class to film it for his show, *Visiting...with Huell Howser.* The theme was that he traveled around California visiting and filming interesting and sometimes little known places and events.

Mr. Howser was extremely cordial to the class and structured us about what he was planning to do. He was so easy-going that everyone felt relaxed. The cameraman started to videotape the session as Howser approached various class members and interviewed them. Half-way through the filming, he walked over to where I was sitting and started asking me some questions.

We had all taped our headshots on the wall in preparation for the filming. Huell–notice we're on a first name basis now–wanted me to go up to the wall and point out my headshot. He asked me about it and about myself.

He was also gracious enough to pose later for a photograph with me snapped by another class member on my trusty camera. When Huell Howser's program finally aired, I was one of the main people interviewed.

With TV Personality, Huell Howser (right),
and my teacher, Buddy Powell (left)

Several months later, I was contacted again by Elizabeth Pope, the same journalist who had written the *Time Magazine* article. This time, she was writing an article entitled "Sing, Paint and Act Your Way to Good Health." It featured seniors who were involved in activities which helped them remain healthy. It was to appear in a special section of the *Los Angeles Times* newspaper entitled, "Living Well, The Senior Years."

Elizabeth Pope planned to interview Barbara Gannen about her senior acting class. She wanted to include a portion about Dad and me as class members.

Dad was delighted. Now, he was going to be in the newspaper, too. When the article came out, there were several paragraphs devoted to us.

Again, Elizabeth interviewed me over the telephone. Here is the portion about Dad and me almost verbatim as it appeared in the article:

Lee Gale Gruen, 64, a retired probation officer...had never acted before joining Gannen's class, but was immediately hooked by the experience.

Four years later she still takes classes, but she's got an agent and paid gigs in commercials, plays and films.

'I feel like a new woman,' she said. 'I'm so much more confident now, and memorizing long scripts keeps me mentally sharp.'...After her mother's death, Gruen invited her father Marvin Schelf, then 85, to join the class to ease his grief.

'He got right up in front of the class and read. By the time we drove home, he was asking what time I'd be picking him up next week.'

Since there were few roles for men his age, Gruen wrote scenes for them to perform together, based on her father's Mr. Magoo-like characteristics. No longer acting, her dad is now in a nursing home, and the last scene they did together, he did from his wheelchair.

'He adored it,' she said of their daughter/father act. 'It became a significant part of his life and he developed quite a following.'

* * *

Dad and I played Gin Rummy at the nursing home. Alice had been the one to suggest it. She mentioned that she had once had a job as the activities director in a nursing home and knew that card playing kept the residents' minds sharp.

I cranked up Dad's hospital bed so he could sit upright, and I sat beside it. I pushed the movable table top over the bed and we used it as our card table. I shuffled and dealt because Dad couldn't do so anymore. He was able to hold the cards, although awkwardly.

He did manage to play the game, but not like his old self. Dad had always been such a good card player. He was sharp and shrewd, and he rarely lost. Now, I often won.

Although he wouldn't have approved, I occasionally let him win. Sometimes, he even won on his own. Dad looked forward to those games. I did, too. I hadn't played that much Gin Rummy in years. It was one of the few activities we could share anymore.

CHAPTER 12
Goodbye Dad

It was almost Dad's 90th birthday. I wanted to do something special for him. He was too weak to leave the nursing home, so it would have to be held there. The head nurse told me about a man who periodically volunteered his time as a host to the residents, announcing birthdays and such. He was very tall and thin, and would show up wearing a tuxedo and carrying balloons. I called him immediately.

Yes, he would host a birthday celebration for Dad. He asked me a bunch of questions about Dad's life so he could talk about him. I told the head nurse to invite all the staff to the party. I bought refreshments for everyone. Of course, I kept it a secret from Dad; it was supposed to be a surprise.

On Dad's birthday, I arrived an hour early. I kissed him and wheeled him onto the patio. Slowly, staff started drifting in. Dad looked around.

"What's going on?"

"What do you mean, Dad?" I answered innocently.

He knew me too well, and he was just too alert. He didn't say anything more, but he had that suspicious look on his face.

The Master of Ceremonies arrived shortly, decked out as promised. He was holding a handful of colorful, helium-filled balloons.

"Did you arrange this?" Dad whispered to me.

He didn't like surprises.

"It's your birthday, isn't it?"

The MC tied the balloons to Dad's wheelchair. Then, he began his spiel. He was great! He mentioned all sorts of things about Dad's life. Dad was the focus of attention and really rallied. Before long, he was telling jokes and acting like Mr. Important.

"I didn't see you laughing at my jokes," he said to one staff member as he pointed to her.

She giggled and flushed a bit. That only brought on more laughter from everyone. Dad could still work a crowd—old and frail be damned.

The only ones in attendance besides me were the members of the nursing home staff. My sister was away on vacation, and Dad's two grandsons were unable to come, living so far away. Of course, they all dutifully called and wished Dad a happy birthday as did his sisters who lived in another State and weren't in good enough health themselves to travel.

**With Dad at His 90th Birthday Party
at the Nursing Home**

After it was all over, I suggested to Dad that I wheel him outside for a while since it was sunny and beautiful. As we proceeded down the street, he said, "How much did you have to pay that guy?"

"What's the difference?"

That was Dad, frugal to the bitter end.

"I just wanted to know."

"Twenty five dollars."

He knew I was lying. It was three times that much.

"You had a good time, didn't you?" I added, irritation in my voice.

"Yes," he answered softly. He didn't bring it up again.

Well, that wasn't the end of that business. A few weeks later when I visited, Dad had instructions for me.

"Go to Marshall's and buy me two sweaters. I saw on TV they're having a sale, two for the price of one. Don't spend a lot. I don't need anything fancy."

Dad never needed anything fancy. He was always saving for the future. That trait was so ingrained in him that he couldn't see that the future for him was now. In his mind, the future never came. Maybe it was a good thing. Although his constant "tightening the belt" got on my nerves, at least he still cared about life in the only way that worked for him.

Over the years, Dad used to call his stock broker, Paul Shannon, regularly. He'd chew Paul out if he were charged the slightest amount too much on commissions or fees.

Paul, wonderful Paul, always listened patiently and handled it, even if sometimes the discrepancy came out of his own commission. That was Dad—you could strangle him, but you still loved him.

When Richard was about to graduate high school, he needed his own car to drive to college which was a significant distance away with no feasible public transportation available. Dad offered to sell Richard his Toyota Corolla, and then planned to buy a new car for himself. As a graduation present, he gave Richard four new tires and a tune up. As my present, I decided to give Richard one fourth the cost of the car. I found a picture of a Toyota Corolla, cut off a fourth of it and put it in a graduation card.

Dad had a long talk with Richard about getting a part-time job so he could make payments of twenty five dollars per month toward what he owed on the car. He structured Richard very carefully about his responsibility.

"I expect the payment to be in my hand on the first day of each month. If, for any reason, you can't make the payment, I want you to call me, explain the problem and make arrangements to pay it by another date."

Dad fashioned a payment record document by hand. He was going to enter every payment he received, the same as a bank loan, and would mail Richard a receipt following each one. This was man-to-man stuff and Richard took it very seriously being trusted as an adult by his grandfather.

Unbeknownst to Richard, Dad opened a separate savings account at the bank into which he deposited each of Richard's payments until the car was paid off. He transferred that account into Richard's name upon his graduation from college and gave Richard the passbook as a graduation gift. The mantle was passing. Dad was teaching the youngest generation in his family the expertise he had to pass on—his knowledge of finances.

For as long as I could remember, even when he lived in a single room at the retirement home, Dad would always sit at his desk making out his bills and reviewing his investment statements—another official role of the head of the family right up there with carving the dinner roast. He had always prided himself so much on handling his own business affairs. In his eyes, his financial acumen was his greatest accomplishment.

Nevertheless, he had taught me how to do it for him years earlier "for when the time comes," he'd say.

It was hard for me to listen. After all, "the time" was always so far in the future; why go through all this?

When Dad started living at the nursing home, the time had finally come. He could no longer handle his own finances. I could barely do it. It was too painful. The first time I sat down to pay his bills, I couldn't do it. I wanted things to be as they'd always been. It was such a major passage and I hated it.

Dad took great pride in never having to go to his children for financial help. The nursing home was extremely expensive, and I paid all the bills out of his bank account. He never asked me how much those bills were. I think he realized that it would just upset his frugal nature if he found out.

"How much am I worth?" he'd ask me every so often.

I'd assure him that he had plenty of money.

"Are you sure?" he'd respond with a worried look.

* * *

Buddy Powell periodically invited guest speakers to his acting class. One day he informed us that a talent agent, Daniel Hoff, would be coming in a few weeks, scouting for senior talent to represent for commercials. I knew that Daniel Hoff was a pretty important agent. In fact, a few years earlier when I was quite new to the acting game, I had even auditioned at his agency.

The Daniel Hoff Agency held open calls about once a month, and actors could come and audition. The one time I had gone, I learned the meaning of the phrase "cattle call." The place was filled with actors, all studying the scripts that had been handed out to them. We were going to be called in one at a time to read our copy while being filmed.

Actors were sitting in the lobby, on the floor, outside the office in the hallway, leaning against the wall near the elevators and practically spilling out of the windows. It felt like about a hundred people were waiting the entire time I was there. As some would get in the elevators to leave, new ones would get out to take their places. It was exciting and anxiety-provoking all at once.

I found a little space on the floor to sit and proceeded to study my script. It was something catchy about some food product. I kept going over and over it. After about an hour, my name was called. I shoved my way up to the name-caller and she showed me where to wait in rotation to go into some as-yet-undisclosed inner sanctum where the audition would take place.

This was another first for me and I was tense. I was stationed just outside a doorway. When it opened, an actor exited and it was my turn. I entered to find a lone woman with a camera on a tripod.

"Okay, go ahead," she instructed.

I didn't know where to look. It's quite disconcerting to have a conversation with a camera lens which, I have come to learn, is what is often expected in auditions.

I said my lines the best I could. She thanked me briskly and made it clear that now I was expected to leave. I couldn't have been in that room for more than thirty seconds.

That was it? That was my big opportunity to prove myself? Whew, and I never even got to see Daniel Hoff.

I never heard from the Daniel Hoff Agency. I guess they had decided they could live without my talents. Now, Hoff himself was coming to one of my senior acting classes. We were all pretty keyed up. Buddy explained that Mr. Hoff would bring a commercial script for us to study. Then, he would videotape each of us delivering the material.

On the big day, the classroom was filled. Buddy had notified the students in all three of his classes and there were about seventy five hopeful, twittering seniors in attendance.

"Daniel Hoff is running late. He'll be here in about an hour," Buddy announced.

We were all gabbing and Buddy couldn't quiet us down. A classroom of seniors is not too different from a classroom of kindergartners. As people age, they seem to regress and become more childlike. This phenomenon was certainly on display that day.

Finally, Hoff made his entrance.

Wait a minute. That's Daniel Hoff? There must be some mistake."

I had built him up so much in my mind that I expected an older distinguished-looking man with a full head of white hair dressed impeccably in a three-piece suit.

Instead, in walked a man dressed in jeans who looked to be in his thirties. He was followed by a dog. Daniel was mild mannered and seemed to be just a regular guy. I couldn't believe it. This casual younger man had built up a large successful talent agency. I was impressed.

The first thing Daniel did was grab a stool and put his jacket on the seat. The dog jumped on top of the jacket and hunkered down—only in L.A.

Daniel passed out the same script to everyone. He explained that he would film each of us individually as we performed the material. After reviewing the footage over the next few weeks, his office would call a select group of us to offer commercial representation.

The noise became deafening as everyone began practicing the lines of copy. Then, it was show time.

Daniel called us, one at a time, to the front of the room. Well, a group of seniors can also be as obnoxious as a group of kindergartners. Everyone was trying to out-perform the next one. After all, this was the big time—no holds barred—go for the jugular—take no prisoners.

When it was my turn, I walked up to the front of the class and handed Daniel my headshot. It was a new one, now in color, which had become the industry standard since the last time I'd auditioned at his agency. Also, I looked quite different this time. Buddy had had another agent as a guest speaker at the class about a year earlier.

"Let your hair grow out to its natural color and go out for older roles. You'll get more work," she advised us.

Well, the men weren't exactly knocking down my door with my blond hair which I had been dying since I was a teenager. I figured I'd go for the acting and to hell with the men.

Slowly, I stopped dying my hair. When it had all grown out, I had a head full of snow white hair, just like Dad's. It took some getting used to as it made me feel a lot older–age appropriate, God forbid–but it was really quite attractive. I also let my natural curls have their way. The majority of my friends liked it a lot, even the skeptics who had warned me against doing it.

I stepped to the mark on the floor where I was supposed to stand while being filmed by Hoff. I was thinking about my experience at his agency those few years earlier.

This is it. One chance to do it right.

It was different this time. Now, I had a couple more years of acting experience under my belt. Also, the atmosphere was much less stressful with Buddy and all of my fellow classmates sitting nearby. I felt very secure. I did my best and walked back to my seat.

I drove directly to Dad's after class. I sat down beside his bed, our usual method of interacting now, and shared the entire Daniel Hoff experience with him.

Dad was pumped up by the whole thing. He was living vicariously through me. I was okay with that. This whole adventure had started out as my gift to him.

Dad and I both spent a nervous few weeks with no word from Daniel Hoff. I finally left for a previously planned vacation in San Antonio, Texas. A few days later, as I was walking with the tour group, my cell phone rang. It was a representative from the Daniel Hoff Talent Agency, offering to represent me.

I called Dad.

"I never doubted you for a minute."

He was also quite sure that he would have been chosen if he had been able to audition. Humble as always, that was Dad.

Each of my accomplishments became Dad's bragging rights. The nursing home staff as well as the sharper residents were regaled daily with my escapades in the weird world of show business.

The Daniel Hoff Agency had chosen about a dozen new senior clients from the audition at Buddy's class. We all met at the talent agency office for orientation given by Daniel himself. He studied each of our headshots and told a few to make changes to their appearance, such as getting a new hairstyle or shaving off a mustache.

With My Commercial Agent, Daniel Hoff

When he got to mine, he liked my hair but wanted me to cut it a bit shorter. However, he wasn't happy with the color of the blouse I was wearing. He wanted me to bring in a variety of blouses for him to see. He also wanted some of the group, including me, to get new headshots taken.

I returned to Daniel's office a few days later with a selection of blouses from my closet in different styles and colors. He settled on one which was not actually my choice. He was right, though. The color really made my eyes stand out.

Most of us needing new headshots went together to a photographer Daniel knew and liked. The price he had arranged for us was extremely reasonable, so we decided to go with his recommendation.

On headshot day, we all showed up at the photographer's studio. We were wired and talking incessantly. Within a short time, a makeup artist arrived courtesy of Daniel Hoff. He had thought so much of us that he was investing some of his time, energy and money in our future as commercial actors.

When it was my turn, the photographer took me into his staging area. It was just a big room with a warehouse-like feel. There were large backdrops leaning against the walls and he moved one into place behind me. He began talking to me and was so calm and reassuring that I immediately relaxed. As he was shooting pictures, he was giving me directions to elicit the look or expression he wanted.

In about an hour, we were finished. The photographer had taken one hundred sixty-eight shots. Before I left, he gave me a CD containing all of them.

My Main Acting Headshot

One of My Character Headshots

Daniel studied all of the photos and he and I settled on one which was to be my main headshot. I took it to the office of the principal internet casting website used by the Hoff Agency where the technician would make the recommended adjustments suggested by Daniel and put my photo online. The agency would then be able to submit me for acting jobs.

Another Character Headshot

I watched as the technician inserted my CD into his computer and realigned my photo courtesy of the Photoshop computer program. My head and neck moved little by little into a more upright position–amazing.

I was appreciative of Daniel's guidance. It felt good to have a professional directing me rather than stumbling along blindly. I had prints made of my new headshot to present at auditions. I was ready.

The very next day, I got a call from the Daniel Hoff Agency. They notified me of my first commercial audition as their client.

* * *

By this time, Dad had been completely bedridden for a few months. I could see that he was steadily getting weaker. He had had pneumonia several times, and so far it had been beaten back with antibiotics. However, the head nurse told me the last time that the doctor had prescribed the strongest antibiotic available as nothing else worked anymore. She warned me that the next time, that one might not work, either.

Dad was still alert and could understand everything I told him, but things were different now. Where he had been so enthusiastic two years earlier when I got my first agent, he was just too weak to show much emotion about my now getting a much better-known one. All he could muster was a little smile. But, he always greeted me with that smile whenever I walked into his room.

"Hi," he would manage to say, barely having the lung power to get it out.

In those final days, if Dad ever thought about dying, and he must have, he never let on. The main discussions we had were about my acting, willing his body to science for research like Mother had done, and getting his financial affairs in order.

"Your father died this morning."

I stared blankly at the telephone receiver. Although I had been anticipating that call, I just couldn't process it.

"I'll be right over," I guess I responded.

It was 5:30 in the morning and I had been sleeping. I pulled on some clothes, stumbled to the car and somehow drove to the nursing home.

I had seen Dad the day before and he was in a coma. I kept up a steady stream of one-sided conversation, not knowing if he could hear me or not. Without warning, his arm shot up and I grabbed his hand. I'm sure he was aware I was there.

After I arrived at the nursing home, I sat with Dad for a long time. I couldn't believe he was dead. He looked so small and used up. I was numb. I had no emotion. I just sat there.

Body Man soon arrived, just like it had happened with Mother. I stood in the doorway watching as he wrapped up Dad's body in a sheet and put him on a gurney. The whole thing felt very clinical to me, as though I weren't a part of it. He wheeled Dad out of the room and down the hall. I watched until he turned a corner and was out of sight.

My father was gone.

CHAPTER 13
I'll Tell Ya, I Could Write a Book

I felt lost and vulnerable after Dad died, like a child. I might as well have been five years old. Now, I had no parents. It's true what they say, "You can be an orphan at any age." Dad had always been my rock–my support. Of course, in his final years, it was really the other way around, but I never saw it like that.

Dad had always insisted he was happy just having two daughters and no sons. Nevertheless, it was obvious that I was his heir designate, taking the role traditionally reserved for a son. He taught me what he had to pass on–his knowledge of finances.

Julie, Mother and I all knew and agreed that I would be the one to handle his affairs when he could no longer do so, and to be the trustee of his estate when he died.

I started the painful process of going through Dad's papers to begin the distribution of his trust. I opened his metal boxes, the ones with all his important papers inside.

While shuffling through one bunch, which included stock account statements, check books, important telephone numbers and such, I came upon a folded, well-worn, sheaf of papers. I opened it and discovered that it was Dad's script from one of our showcase scenes with his handwritten notes. Well, that stopped me cold. I couldn't continue. I needed a break. It lasted a week.

Being the trustee of Dad's estate took months. I kept coming upon new discoveries. I found an old ledger he had kept of his stocks dating back to 1946. I was only five years old at the time.

Dad had been investing that long?

There were a lot of blank pages in the ledger, and I saw that he had used some of them to make himself a daily calendar for 2004. That was Dad, a stock trader and recycler all in one.

For years, I used to save the coupon section from the Sunday edition of the *Los Angeles Times* newspaper. I'd bring it to Dad the next time I saw him. He loved to shop for all the bargains and would buy stuff he and Mother didn't even want or couldn't use, just because he got it on sale. Mother used to rant about it, all to no avail.

After Dad moved to the retirement home and even to the nursing home, he still wanted me to save the coupon section for him. Although he no longer did any food shopping, he got brownie points by giving it to the staff members—always the finagler.

Now, each Sunday when I rifle through the newspaper, separating the parts I want to read from those I don't, I come upon the coupon section and quickly pass it by. It hurts too much to look at it.

* * *

While Dad and I had still been attending acting class, I started thinking about what an interesting book our story would make. Then, I'd get busy with acting and other things in my life and soon forget about it. Months later, it would pop into my head again and I'd dismiss it just as fast.

I hadn't consciously thought about the book for at least a few years. One night, I woke up with my head bursting with thoughts.

Oh God, it's 3:00 am," I noticed, glancing at the clock with one eye open and the other shut.

I had the entire framework for this book mapped out in my head along with the chapter headings, the opening line and countless individual sentences and paragraphs. Apparently, my creative juices had been cooking stealthily and chose that moment to boil over. I tried to push the thoughts out of my mind and go back to sleep, telling myself that I'd handle it in the morning. No deal. I was wide awake and new lines and refinements kept emerging. Even worse, two voices were dialoguing in my head.

"*I'm out of the bottle now, honey, and I'm not going back,*" said my creative genie.

I tried to reason with Genie:

Me: I'll make a deal with you. You can come back in the morning after I get some sleep.

Genie: No way. I'm running things now.

Me: Give me a break.

Genie: Why?

Me: Because I'm a nice person.

Genie: Tough.

There was nothing to be done but write down my thoughts on whatever paper I could muster. However, I was not about to give in to sleep-interruption by getting out of bed and walking down the hallway to my desk to search for proper paper. So, my first stab at writing a book was composed entirely on Post-it notes while sitting on the edge of my bed in the wee hours of the morning.

This went on for two hours. Each time I tried to go back to sleep, my head would start swimming with new thoughts and I'd have to turn on the light, sit up and resume writing.

I wrote on the front and back of the darn things. Did you know that you can write on the sticky part of Post-its? (I'll bet you're going to try it.) That's not something I had really wanted to learn in my lifetime. A few hours later, I had Post-its scattered all over the floor. By the time I was finished, my hand resembled a crab and I couldn't feel it anymore. Why couldn't I be the kind of writer who methodically gets up at the same time each morning, walks into her office and just sits down and writes for a given length of time? Noooo, I had to lose sleep over my literary gems. If that's what is meant by the creative process, it sucks.

The next morning, I sat down at my computer and typed up everything from my Post-it notes. I wanted Dad to be able to read what I had written of the book so far.

Although I only had a rough draft of the first three chapters, I brought them over to him. I watched as he was reading, worried about his reaction, especially to the not-so-flattering parts. He laughed occasionally but showed no other emotion. When he was finished, he handed the pages back to me and just said softly, "very good." I couldn't tell if he didn't like it or was just too weak to say anything else.

I decided to buy a tape recorder so that if I woke up in the middle of the night again, I could just reach over without getting out of bed and record my thoughts. I was making progress. However, the first time I tried it I discovered that I had to turn on the light to see the buttons on the tape recorder, thereby waking myself up and defeating the purpose.

I was still doing my best research in my sleep. However, at least my modus operandi had improved. Instead of awakening in the dark hours, I slept soundly but woke up closer to dawn, head overflowing with ideas. I seemed to do better jotting them down on paper rather than dictating them into the tape recorder. The act of writing seemed to help me organize my thoughts more than verbalizing them.

Memories would also drift into my consciousness while I was driving. I'd have to pull the car over, park and write them down. After the first time it happened, I stocked the car with pencils and pads of paper. It's funny how, in this modern world of technology, the ancient method of setting quill to parchment is still the best.

I never really did anything further with my efforts to that point. After Dad died, I just put the book out of my mind. It was too upsetting to think about—better to just concentrate on my acting.

My little part-time second career had started to take over my life. I've auditioned for such diverse roles as biker granny and Mrs. Claus. I typically get cast in roles like grandmother, wealthy socialite, sexy senior, etc. However, I have played against type: gangster granny, granny rapper, homeless woman.

You never know what you're going to encounter with acting jobs. On one of those "homeless woman" roles, I found myself working as a featured background player in the middle of the night, outside, in the skid row area of downtown Los Angeles. The wardrobe department gave me a big overcoat to wear, which was several sizes too large.

"Use no makeup on her," the director barked to the makeup artist.

That was like a dagger into my ribs. I was going to go without makeup–au naturel–oh no.

"Do something with her hair," he also commanded.

My naturally-curly hair usually looks neat and beauty shop ready on its own without my having to do much to it. The hair stylist used a hair-pressing iron to straighten some of my curls and make them stick out at odd angles, causing me to look more downtrodden.

After hours of arranging the shoot area and placing all the actors in position, I was now seated on a bus bench. A water truck hired by the production company drove down the street spraying water over the pavement and sidewalks to make it look as though it had just rained. Any curly-head will immediately understand what humidity in the air does to naturally curly hair. All my newly-straightened locks instantly sprang back to their original location.

The director and hair stylist both ran over to me like a racing team in tandem. They looked at each other and rolled their eyes.

"Whatever," the director sighed, throwing up his hands.

A homeless woman who looked like she had just stepped out of a beauty parlor was going to be in the scene.

At 5:00 am, the shoot was finished. I returned to the lot where I had parked my car, exhausted and very ready to go home. Then, I noticed something was not quite right. My driver's side window was broken.

Although the lot was supposed to be watched over by a security guard hired by the production company, thieves had managed to break the windows of several cars parked there. After some careful inspection, I found that nothing had been stolen. The director promised to pay for the repair of my broken window, so I finally drove home, with cold air blowing in my face.

I have only worked a few times as a background player. I didn't really care for it. The pay is low and the hours are long. There is a lot of down-time where most of the actors just sit around trading war stories. It's fun for a while, but soon becomes tiresome.

Conditions for background players are not always very good, either. When I worked on the job in skid row, provisions were brought in to feed the cast and crew dinner. The background players got pizza, while the technical crew was served gourmet food. Each group was segregated in different sections of the vacant lot that served as our waiting area, although we could still see each other. It smacked of old Southern discrimination scenarios. The background players were on one side eating their pizza, while the crew was on the other side enjoying its fancy fare.

When everyone had finished eating, the background players were invited to eat whatever was left over of the crew's food. Of course, by that time we'd already filled up on pizza. Thanks a lot! It all has something to do with union vs. non-union jobs. However you cut it, it's the pits and I decided that was not for me.

To date, I have appeared in numerous commercials, some for prominent products. They have been shown on various media including local television, national television and the Internet. A few years ago, some friends traveling in Europe saw one of my commercials there on CNN.

I have been in several small roles on cable television. One of my first television jobs was in 2007 on the History Channel–a program about the end of the world. I played Sybil, the ancient oracle of Rome who predicted centuries into the future that the world would end around 2012. A short clip of the program including my part was on YouTube for a while, and it had over five million hits before it was removed.

The shoot was a low budget project and the wardrobe staff simply made my costume by draping yardage material around my body and as a veil on my head. My sandals were made out of cardboard with laces stapled to them. However, walking around the rocky cave terrain in the Hollywood Hills where the program was filmed caused the sandals to break. I hadn't worn any appropriate shoes to the shoot as I knew I'd be given a costume. So, I had to wear my white socks and clunky black, Mary Jane style walking shoes. The director said he just wouldn't shoot my feet. Nevertheless, in the finished product, there were a few seconds showing my feet complete with the shoes and socks—totally out of sync with my Roman style clothing.

Once, I appeared on network television in a well-known soap opera, General Hospital. I had two lines, one of which ended up on the cutting room floor. But, hey, one also aired.

I have done community theater plays, music videos, magazine print jobs, voice-over jobs, and short films. I am in the actors' union. I even taught an Acting-for-Fun class on a cruise ship.

Some of the stranger things I have done as an actress are: dressed in a space suit, ridden a mechanical horse, fallen onto an air mattress, and worn a rubber suit which added about 200 pounds to my frame.

For several years I have worked periodically at the UCLA Medical School portraying various patients. It's a program that teaches patient-interviewing skills to medical students.

A few years ago, I was one of six background exercise/dancers on the Jane Fonda Prime Time Firm & Burn workout DVD. I also participated in a Miss Fitness Pageant in the over-forty category. I was the oldest one there and won a medal for Miss

Congeniality–eat your heart out Sandra Bullock. I hung my medal on my hallway wall as part of my acting rogues gallery. Although not technically from an acting job, it felt right–part of my new life.

I now have so many entrees for my resume that I must pick and choose what to include. It's so different from when I only had roles from my acting class showcases to list and had to arrange them carefully to fill up the blank spaces. I still can't believe I've gotten to this point.

My acting rogues gallery still has wall space. I'll add to it as I get new photos, posters and mementos of the acting work I do. And, of course, I'll share it all with Dad.

Oh no, I can't do that anymore.

I frequently find myself ready to share things with Dad. Richard became an attorney after a grueling stint in law school. My first reaction was to call Dad and tell him.

Oh, no, I thought for the hundredth time, *I can't.*

Dad was still alive when Richard started law school. He was always encouraging and supportive of him. He would have been so proud and commandeered full bragging rights. I can almost hear him.

"Well, I'll just run it by my grandson–ah, the lawyer."

Mate and Checkmate.

Recently, I started thinking about the book again. Maybe enough time had gone by since Dad died. I dug out my old notes. New thoughts started coming to the forefront of my mind. I began waking up in the middle of the night with whole passages and anecdotes in my head. Here we go again.

* * *

"Hi Mom, what are you doing?" my son usually opens with when he calls.

"Working on my book, honey," I often respond these days.

I have stepped into my mother's shoes. How many years ago had I called her asking the same question?

"Working on my autobiography, honey," she'd answer.

As we read from it at her memorial service, will my son read from my book one day at mine?

My inspiration for this book was Dad himself. He was such fertile soil. There had been so many "Dad" incidents down through the years. As a child, they weren't so precious. They were upsetting, embarrassing and humiliating. A child sees things through his own immature prism. As an adult, I saw Dad through different eyes. He was a unique man who hurtled through life like a geologic force, depositing gold nuggets for me to mine. At least he got to see a portion of my tribute to him.

Now, I have taken my father's place and moved up to that final rung on the ladder—the oldest, living generation in the family.

Richard married his girlfriend, Debra, and they moved to another State. They now have three beautiful children. Being a grandmother is an incredible experience. I have long talks on the telephone with them all and visit whenever I can.

My nephew, David, has two lovely children, making me a great aunt, also. I'm sorry that Dad never had a chance to meet all of his great-grandchildren.

Just as my father was there for me, I try to be there for my children. I don't always feel like being the oldest living generation. I guess Dad didn't, either. We are thrust into that role kicking and screaming and we can't go back.

"Oh Daddy, I miss you."

www.LeeGaleGruen.com

www.AdventuresWithDadTheBook.com

Email Address:
GowerGulch@yahoo.com

ABOUT THE AUTHOR

Lee Gale Gruen (she uses "Lee Gale" as her first name) has lived in Los Angeles, California since childhood. She has two children and three grandchildren. She graduated college from UCLA and had a 37-year career as a Probation Officer. After retiring, she became a professional actress. Since then, she has appeared in television, commercials, short films, community theater, music videos, voice-overs, print jobs, and live, interactive roles. She performs regularly portraying patients at UCLA Medical School as part of student training. She was one of six supporting exercise/dancers in the 2011 Jane Fonda Prime Time Firm & Burn workout DVD, and was the oldest contestant in a Miss Fitness pageant where she won the Miss Congeniality award. Her transition to becoming an actress in her senior years has been written about in *Time Magazine* and the *Los Angeles Times* newspaper. Lee Gale volunteers as a tour guide at the world famous La Brea Tar Pits. She is currently working on her next book of memoir short stories. Lee Gale is proof of how senior programs and classes can change your life. She is available to speak about her book and as an advocate for senior community programs.

BOOK CLUB
DISCUSSION QUESTIONS

1. Are Baby Boomers and seniors vital members of the community? Do they contribute to the general welfare? How?

2. Should colleges, community centers and other institutions offer classes and programs for Baby Boomers and seniors?

3. How do Baby Boomers and seniors benefit from staying active and engaged? How do those close to them benefit? How does society benefit?

4. Why was the father in the book such an angry, insecure man? Discuss his relationship with his own father.

5. What is the stereotypical First Generation (naturalized foreign born) experience and the Second Generation (children of those parents) experience in the United States...in other countries? Discuss the similarities, differences and conflicts between the First and Second Generations. Is this different from parents and children both born in the same country?

6. What is the father/daughter dynamic in this memoir? Discuss parent/child dynamics in general.

7. Why was the author's sister never able to forgive their father?

8. What is the common thread running through all the acting class, comedy scenes that the author wrote? How do those comedy scenes relate to the author's real-life relationship with her father?

9. Why was the author willing to do anything she could to keep her father alive? Discuss the impact on a child of the loss of a parent. What are the similarities and differences depending on the child's age?

10. What was the attraction between the author's father and mother? How did their personality types influence her?

11. How did the author's mentally challenged child impact her life? How did her normal child impact her life?

12. Discuss how insecurity can manifest itself in opposite behaviors: always wanting to call attention to yourself versus never wanting to call attention to yourself. Why would an insecure person be attracted to acting?